SAINSBU

THE COOKING OF
SPAIN

ELISABETH LUARD

CONTENTS

Published exclusively for J Sainsbury plc
Stamford House Stamford Street
London SE1 9LL
by Martin Books
Simon & Schuster Consumer Group
Fitzwilliam House 32 Trumpington Street
Cambridge CB2 1QY

ISBN 0 85941 691 7

First published April 1991
Second impression October 1991

Printed in Italy by Printer Trento

THE AUTHOR

Sally Soames/Times Newspapers Ltd

As the daughter of a family of career diplomats, Elisabeth Luard spent much of her childhood abroad and grew up a fluent linguist, notably in Spanish and French.

Professionally trained in catering at the Eastbourne School of Domestic Economy, she went to live in southern Spain as a young married woman with her husband and four children. Fifteen years later, after an intervening spell in France and travels throughout most of Europe, she returned to Britain.

A lifelong student of the history of cooking, she began to write on food at the instigation of the deputy editor of the *Spectator*. The appearance of her award-winning and highly acclaimed book, *European Peasant Cookery*, won her a place amongst the top cookery writers. Two of her more recent books, *The Barricaded Larder* and *European Festival Food*, have confirmed this success. She is currently contributing cookery editor of *Country Living* and has a weekly column in the *Scotsman*.

Elisabeth Luard now lives in London but continues to travel widely. She is married to the writer, Nicholas Luard.

INTRODUCTION

Behind the Spain of the tourist resorts, the sea and sand of the Mediterranean beaches, any observant visitor will be aware of older traditions: hilltop villages shaded by Roman-planted olive trees; a sea-horizon sparkling with the lights of wooden fishing boats night-trawling out of ancient ports whose jetties may have been thrown up by Phoenician sailors; rice paddies watered by Moorish irrigation systems. These are the raw materials for the culinary traditions of the real Spain.

As a young housewife in the Andalucían seaport of Tarifa, which for twelve years was my local market town, I learnt that the Spanish menu begins in the market place. By ten o'clock of a morning Tarifa knew what to expect of its day's rations. If the butcher had had a delivery of young beef from the Cadiz bull-ranchers, that evening the town's earthenware cooking-pots filled the air with scented steam from a thousand tomato-rich stews, wafting through the open doorways on whose whitewashed doorsteps all southern dwellers sit on a warm evening to watch the world go by.

When the local fishing boats came in with a particularly fine haul of silvery sardines or purple-tinged clams, or the tuna fish were running through the Straits on a spring tide, the breeze carried a different flavour. Then the frying-pans breathed sea-scents tinged with the sharp tang of the sherry in which the shellfish are left to open, and the rich fruity olive oil which Spaniards, whenever they can afford it, use for frying and saucing their plentiful sea-harvest.

Magnificent seasonal fruit is available everywhere, and the new crop of oranges or the first delivery of grapes is always greeted with delight. Vegetables – at their best when they have been gathered and taken to market that same morning – and salads are usually presented as a separate course before the meat. Otherwise they are included as an integral part of a one-pot meal, of which Spain has a wide variety, mostly based on one of the pulses. Chicken – the small farmer's favourite meat – and wild game are stewed with vegetables in Asturias; in Cataluña they are served in a sauce thickened with nuts; in Seville duck is prepared with sophisticated eastern spicing – a relic of the Moorish caliphs' long sojourn in Andalucía; from the north-east comes a classic winter dish of partridges cooked with cabbage. Eggs are particularly imaginatively treated in the Spanish kitchen, and the sleight of hand needed to turn out a perfect juicy potato omelette is acquired by every young country girl at her mother's elbow.

The Moors, evicted from Granada in 1492 after seven centuries of dominance, and the influx of vegetables from the New World, were the last major influences on the Spanish table. Since then, the regional cookery of Iberia has remained virtually isolated, snug behind its barrier of the Pyrenees, from the fashions and changing tastes which have affected the rest of Europe. Instead Spain has preferred to concentrate on perfecting her own native ingredients and culinary methods.

The strength of Spanish cookery lies in good raw materials that are simply and skilfully prepared. The Spaniard likes his food to be recognisably itself, without too much complication and addition: meats are preferred sauced with their own juices; fish and shellfish are prized if they taste of the sea. The best and freshest in the market is prepared quite simply, but in harmony with the three most important ingredients in the Spanish kitchen: the pure juice of the olive, one of the healthiest oils; wine, most flavoursome of stocks; and garlic, the most aromatic of pot-herbs. From the hot plains of Castile to the cold uplands of the Basque country, from the orange groves of Seville to the granite uplands of Galícia, each region has its own specialities.

BASIC INGREDIENTS

OLIVE OIL

The rich juice of the olive defines the flavour of Spanish cookery. An indigenous crop gathered from trees first planted by the colonising Romans, it is used not only for frying and to dress salads, but also to enrich and season slow-cooked stews. Spain's production is geared to bulk rather than individual small growers. Three grades of olive oil are defined: 'virgin', which is the uncooked, untreated juice (my own favourite, I love the peppery, leafy flavour of green olive oil); 'refined', which is rectified virgin olive oil, usually treated because it has too high an acid level; and that bearing the simple label 'olive oil', which is a mixture of the virgin and the refined. There are no rules, but I use the cheaper – refined – for frying, and the virgin oil, or the mixture, for other purposes.

SALT

The salt-flats of Cadiz have been valued since prehistoric times as a source of sea salt. The Spanish housewife likes her salt rough, grainy and unbleached. The crisp crystals give a slight crunch to a salad and to the batter for frying, and a special character to the bread.

JAMÓN SERRANO

Spanish 'mountain ham' is salt-cured and wind-dried without the application of heat or smoke. Along with olive oil, it is the most valued of flavouring ingredients in Spanish cookery. The closest equivalent is Italian prosciutto, which can be substituted for *jamón serrano*. Flavour and body are more important than tenderness. The best cuts of ham are sliced off finely to be served as they are. The well-flavoured chewy little bits near the bone are used to flavour soups, sauces and croquettes, or they might be fried with eggs, or used to flavour a thick, juicy omelette; while the bones are sawn up to add richness, along with a piece of creamy yellow ham fat, to a bean stew.

CHORIZO

This paprika-spiced sausage is eaten fresh or dried, in which case it is sliced thinly and eaten raw, or it is used to enrich and flavour a stew. *Chorizo* is made with those meaty bits of the household pig which do not go for ham or bacon, prepared in tandem with *jamón serrano*. It is wind-dried and sometimes lightly smoked. *Chorizo* either comes in single lengths, or in long loops, or knotted into short fat links. When the *chorizo* is well-cured (firm and dark) it is enjoyed as it is, like Italian salami, which can be substituted, with a pinch of paprika, if *chorizo* is not available. The softer, less-cured sausages can be grilled whole or sliced and fried with eggs. When making a Spanish stew, black pepper, paprika, cumin, coriander seeds, a splash of red wine, a little garlic and oregano, plus an all-pork sausage will help to reproduce the flavour. Or any pure-pork, paprika-seasoned dried sausage can be substituted.

GARLIC

There are those who love the Mediterranean's most popular flavouring, and those who hate it. Its perfume is unmistakeable, and I belong unashamedly to its devotees. Spanish garlic is relatively mild and sweet, and the cooks of Iberia get through a prodigious amount of it. Be careful not to burn the garlic though: it should never be more than gently caramelised. Garlic-pressers are not a standard item in the Spanish kitchen. I don't much like them either: to my palate, the process seems to produce a bitter mush, instead of that delectable sharp bite. Instead, mash the clove in a pestle and mortar, or use a knife to chop or slice it finely. Family cooks (and me among them) use the aromatic bulb to help cure everything, from hangovers to the common cold.

SPICES AND HERBS

Moorish spicing outlived the re-conquest of 1492: saffron, pepper, coriander seeds, cumin, nutmeg, cloves and cinnamon are still much

Gazpacho (Iced tomato soup, page 22)

Paella (Saffron rice, page 58)

Tortilla Española (Spanish potato omelette, page 26)

Flan (Caramel custard, page 94)

Sardinas Asadas (Grilled sardines, page 14)

used today. The New World contributed chocolate, vanilla and, most important, paprika; dried red peppers are also stored, to be torn up and stirred into the cooking pot.

WINE IN COOKING

It is the dry white wines of the south – sherry, manzanilla and the wines of Montilla – which are the most used in Spanish cookery. Many Andalucían recipes use a glass of dry sherry, or local sherry-type wine, as a cooking broth or in a marinade. The sweet wines of Malaga, and Jerez' sweet sherries, are lovely with desserts. They are good, too, to add depth to gravy.

OLIVES

Olives are the classic *tapa*, used as the foundation for a glass of wine. Spain's olive pickling industry exports its anchovy- and pimento-stuffed, cured green olives all over the world. Olives for pickling are gathered while still green, before they ripen to black, the stage at which they are pressed for oil. They are cracked, leached and then preserved in brine: flavourings include herbs, garlic and wine vinegar, and sometimes chilli and lemon or bitter orange. Canned olives can be given a lift by such a marination.

SHERRY VINEGAR

Not something any cellarman likes to admit to, but the fashion for Italian balsamic vinegar has alerted the sherry-men to the potential of an excellent product, until now quietly kept for home use. Look out for it: it is delicious, with a rich oaky flavour; but it must be used sparingly, as it is strong. Balsamic or red or white wine vinegar can be used if you cannot get it.

CHEESE

Spain has a suprisingly wide range of cheeses, from the simplest of fresh curds to sophisticated matured, blue-veined cheeses. These are prized in their own right, and are not often used in traditional Spanish cookery. *Manchego,* the

Note on quantities

All recipes in this book give ingredients in both metric (g, ml, etc.) and imperial (oz, pints, etc.) measures. Use either set of quantities, but not both, in any one recipe.

All teaspoons and tablespoons are level, unless otherwise stated. 1 teaspoon = a 5 ml spoon; 1 tablespoon = a 15 ml spoon.

Egg size is medium (size 3), unless otherwise stated.

Coarse salt and freshly ground pepper should be used for salt and pepper throughout.

Preparation and cooking times

Preparation and cooking times are included at the head of the recipes as a general guide; preparation times, especially, are approximate and timings are usually rounded to the nearest 5 minutes.

Preparation times include the time taken to prepare ingredients in the list, but not to make any 'basic' recipe.

The cooking times given at the heads of the recipes denote cooking periods when the dish can be left largely unattended, e.g. baking, stewing, and not the total amount of cooking for the recipe. Always read and follow the timings given for the steps of the recipe in the method.

most widely-known, is a matured hard cheese made from ewe's milk on the high plateau of La Mancha; it is used on *gratins* and in croquettes. Mature Cheddar is the closest substitute.

ALMONDS

The Moors planted Spain's almond groves with stock from the Jordan valley. They found the fertile plain of Granada ideal for the cultivation of their favourite nut tree. As a result, almonds are used extensively in the Spanish kitchen, both whole and ground, in sweetmeats and to thicken sauces. The Christmas *turrón* is a delectable almond and honey sweetmeat directly decended from the Arab *halva*. My own favourites are the sandy-textured *Turrón de Jijona*, and *Turrón de Alicante*, a crackable nougat studded with toasted almonds. In addition there are various marzipans, including varieties studded with crystallised fruit or covered with chocolate, and dust-soft shortbreads made with ground almonds.

BREAD

Spanish bread is excellent, and many villages still boast a baker to supply the most important staple of the rural diet. Close-textured and creamy-white, with a crisp golden crust, country bread is usually sour-dough, with each batch raised with a starter from the day or week before. This, plus the precise mix and milling of the flour, and even the wood used to heat the oven, gives an individual flavour to the product of different bakeries.

LARD

Manteca, pure pork lard, is used in baking and to enrich stews and sauces instead of butter, which is not a traditional ingredient in Spanish cooking. It comes in three flavours: plain white for pastry and shortbread; red (*colorada*), with garlic, herbs and paprika, to add sparkle to a bean stew; and a paprika-coloured dripping in which pieces of meat are preserved – rather like French *rilletes* – which is delicious on bread.

TAPAS

A strong tradition of communal eating and hospitality has led to the pleasurable Spanish habit of dropping in to the local bar for *tapas* – that is, a doll-sized portion of the house speciality, offered on a tiny plate as the free 'cover' for a glass of wine. In the little *ventas* of rural districts this can be as simple as a dish of home-pickled olives, a slice of spicy *chorizo* sausage or a nugget of the local cheese.

In large cities, the browsing population will stroll from one bar to another, sampling the company and cooking of each. Although this delightful habit is now under threat, the habit of taking 'something to pick' is not. The tiny individual *tapa* is today being replaced by a full or half 'ration' of a dish which is shared between friends as an appetiser with a glass of red wine, or, more traditionally, chilled dry sherry.

CROQUETAS DE JAMÓN

Ham croquettes — Serves 6

Preparation time: 20 minutes + 1 hour chilling + 25 minutes cooking

For the filling:

- *5 tablespoons olive oil or 125 g (4 oz) margarine*
- *4 heaped tablespoons plain flour*
- *600 ml (1 pint) chicken stock or milk, or a mixture of water and sherry*
- *2–4 tablespoons finely chopped ham, preferably serrano*
- *1 heaped tablespoon chopped fresh parsley*
- *1 teaspoon dried marjoram*
- *1 teaspoon paprika*

Cheap and delicious, sometimes made only with a good strong broth, croquettes are a standard of the tapa menu. The skill lies in achieving a delicately crisp exterior enclosing a creamy piquant interior. If you want to make large quantities, or have trouble rolling the mixture and coating it – and it is a bit temperamental – include a leaf of gelatine in the broth, so that the filling sets more firmly, and freeze the little cylinders before coating and frying them. The more skilful you become, the softer you can make the filling, and the more delicate the croquettes will be.

Heat the oil or margarine in a saucepan. Stir in the flour and let it froth up for a moment. Remove from the heat and beat the liquid in gradually with a wooden spoon. Cook over a gentle heat until you have a very thick, soft

½ teaspoon grated nutmeg

salt and pepper

For the coating:

3–4 tablespoons seasoned plain flour

1 egg, beaten with 2 tablespoons milk

250 g (8 oz) toasted breadcrumbs

oil for frying

sauce. Stir in the ham, parsley, marjoram, paprika and nutmeg. Season to taste with salt and pepper. Spread the mixture on a plate and cover with an inverted plate. Leave to cool and firm for an hour or two, overnight if possible.

Spread the flour on one plate, the egg-and-milk on a second and the breadcrumbs on a third. With a knife, mark the filling mixture into 20–25 short stubby fingers. Form each into a neat cylinder. Roll each cylinder first in the flour, then in the egg mixture, and finally press it firmly into the breadcrumbs. All surfaces should be well coated or the croquette will burst into the oil. Continue until the sauce is used up.

Heat 2.5 cm (1 inch) of oil in a frying pan. When it is hot, slip in the croquettes a few at a time – not too many or the oil temperature will drop. Fry them for 4–5 minutes until crisp and golden brown. Drain on kitchen paper.

Serve the croquettes piping hot, with a glass of very cold sherry to cool your tongue.

PAN CON TOMATE

Bread with tomato — Serves 4

Preparation time: 5–10 minutes

4 thick slices of close-textured bread, preferably home-made

1 garlic clove, halved

1 beef tomato, halved

2 tablespoons virgin olive oil

Good bread and the best olive oil are the essence of this simplest of tapas, to be served as a nibble with a glass of chilled dry sherry or red wine. Bread with garlic and olive oil is also a favourite field-worker's breakfast. Garlic lovers may prefer to chop the garlic finely and spread it over the bread.

Toast the bread if it is not absolutely fresh.

Rub each slice of bread or toast with the cut garlic clove and the tomato. If you prefer a thicker layer of tomato, grill and mash up the tomato first. Cut each slice of bread into four and finish with a trickle of olive oil.

Top any leftovers with grated cheese and a sprinkle of herbs, and pop them under the grill.

SARDINAS ASADAS

Grilled sardines (Pictured on page 9) Serves 4

Preparation and cooking time: 15–20 minutes

500 g (1 lb) sardines

1 tablespoon salt

To serve:

lemon quarters

Sardines are cheap and plentiful even in Spain's inland markets: Spanish housewives expect their fish to be perfectly fresh and enjoy the taste of the sea. Sardines are a fine-flavoured fish with plenty of their own fat, and so best prepared as simply as possible.

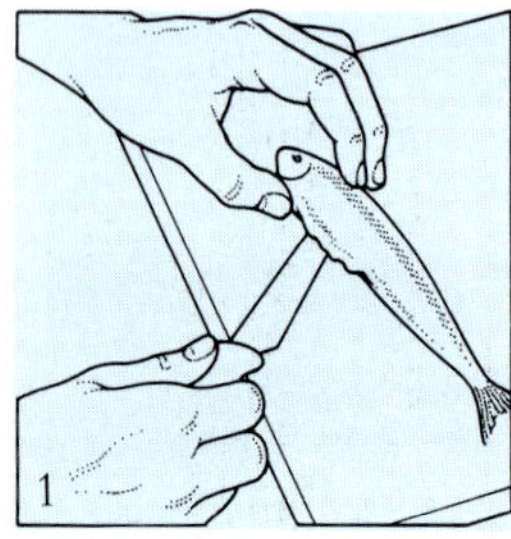

1

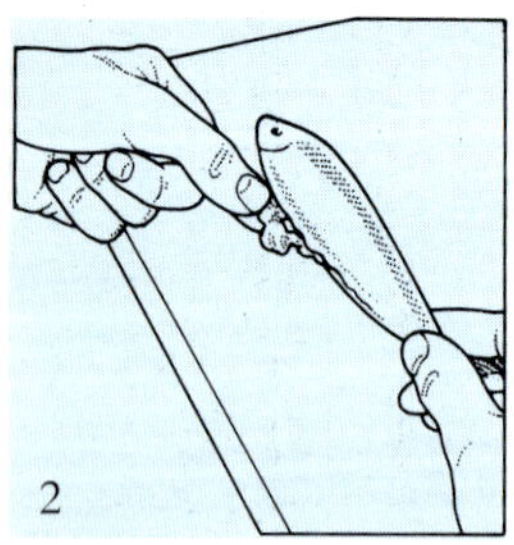

2

Gut the sardines with your index finger or a knife through the soft bellies (1 and 2). (If you are sure the fish is really fresh, this attention is not necessary.) Leave the heads and scales on, and sprinkle the fish with plenty of salt.

Grill the sardines under or over a very fierce heat, turning the fish once. As soon as the skin blisters black and bubbly, they are ready. The thicker the fish the longer they will need: 3–4 minutes on each side is usually ample. Serve with lemon quarters and bread.

SOBRASADA

Chorizo spread Serves 6

Preparation time: 15 minutes

250 g (8 oz) chorizo sausage, skinned and chopped or sliced

100 g (3½ oz) pure, white rendered pork dripping or lard

1 tablespoon paprika

This savoury spread, a kind of soft pork pâté, is a speciality of Mallorca. These days it has become popular all over Spain.

Mash all the ingredients thoroughly together with a fork. This can also be done in a food processor, which will give a smoother texture. Pot and store in the fridge for up to 3 months.

1 tablespoon chopped fresh marjoram or oregano

1 tablespoon sherry vinegar

1 teaspoon salt

½ teaspoon pepper

Bring back to room temperature before serving. It is delicious in toasted sandwiches.

BOQUERONES EN VINAGRE

Little pickled fish — Serves 6–8

Preparation time: 20–30 minutes + 2 days marinating

500 g (1 lb) fresh small sardines, sprats or anchovies

2 large garlic cloves, sliced finely

150 ml (¼ pint) sherry vinegar or wine vinegar

4 tablespoons water if necessary

1 tablespoon olive oil

1 tablespoon chopped fresh parsley

salt and pepper

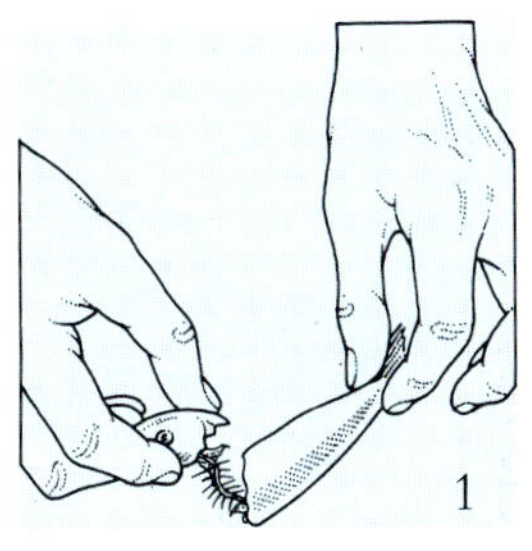
1

Before the days of refrigeration, fish which could not be consumed immediately was either salted or preserved in vinegar. Anchovies are the most plentiful catch: cheap and delicious, every tapa bar round the southern coast of Spain has a dish of them on the menu.

Wash the fish. If using sardines or sprats, check them for scales. Gut the little fish with your finger through the soft belly (see opposite). Then pull the head of each fish firmly down through the belly towards the tail (1). The backbone and whiskery little bones will come out cleanly, leaving the fish split in a butterfly. Lay flesh upwards in a single layer in a shallow dish (2). Sprinkle with the garlic and salt and pepper. If using sherry vinegar, mix it with the water and pour over; wine vinegar can be added as it is. Cover with foil and leave in the fridge to marinate for a day or two.

When ready to serve, finish with the olive oil and parsley. Serve one fish per *tapa*, with a few chunks of fresh bread.

2

ASADILLO

Baked peppers and tomatoes

Serves 4

Preparation time: 20–25 minutes + 20–30 minutes cooking

3 tablespoons olive oil
2 red peppers
2 garlic cloves, chopped
2 beef tomatoes, sliced
1 tablespoon chopped fresh marjoram or oregano or 1 teaspoon dried
salt and pepper

This is a cheerful dish from La Mancha, where it is served as a starter while the main course is cooking. It is lovely warm or cold and keeps well in a screw-top jar in the fridge. It should be brought up to room temperature before serving.

Preheat the oven to Gas Mark 8/230°C/450°F. Oil a shallow casserole.

Roast the peppers over a gas flame or under the grill until the skin blisters black (the kitchen fills with the most delicious aroma). Skin and de-seed the peppers and then cut them into strips.

Arrange the peppers, garlic and tomatoes in layers, seasoning as you do so. Sprinkle with the rest of the oil and the marjoram or oregano. Bake in the oven for 20–30 minutes, until all the flavours are married and the juices reduced.

Serve on squares of bread, or with bread for mopping it up yourself.

Asadillo (Baked peppers and tomatoes)

Anchoas en Conserva con Tomate (Fillets of anchovy with tomato)

Chicoria con Queso de Cabrales (Chicory boats)

ANCHOAS EN CONSERVA CON TOMATE

Fillets of anchovy with tomato — Serves 4

Preparation time: 5–10 minutes

- *50 g (2 oz) can of anchovies in oil*
- *8–12 small rounds of fresh or toasted bread, e.g. baguette*
- *8–12 fine slices of tomato*
- *8–12 capers*
- *1 tablespoon olive oil*
- *pepper*

Salted anchovies are still sold from the barrel in many village stores in Spain; they have a very pungent flavour and need soaking and boning before serving. Canned anchovies do not need such attention and can be served simply on bread, or, as here, with tomato to cut the saltiness.

Check the anchovies for whiskery bones. On a plate, lay a round of bread for each fillet. Top each round with a slice of tomato, a curl of anchovy and a caper. Dress with the oil from the can, the extra olive oil and a sprinkle of pepper.

CHICORIA CON QUESO DE CABRALES

Chicory boats — Serves 4

Preparation time: 10 minutes

- *8 chicory leaves*
- *125 g (4 oz) blue cheese, e.g. Cabrales, Roquefort, Danish blue or Stilton*
- *1 tablespoon anís or anis-flavoured white brandy, or vodka plus ½ teaspoon aniseeds (optional)*
- *2 tablespoons soured cream*
- *1 teaspoon paprika*
- *8 walnut halves*

This delicious little tapa is a speciality of the bars in the north of Spain. The local blue cheese is Cabrales, a chalky-textured, matured cheese made in Asturias in much the same way as French Roquefort.

Wipe the chicory leaves and lay them on a plate. Work the cheese with the brandy or vodka and aniseeds, if used, and soured cream. Fill the boat-shaped leaves with the mixture. Finish with a sprinkle of paprika and a walnut half each.

FIRST-COURSE SOUPS AND SALADS

A light soup or a mixed salad is often served as the first course in Spain. The soup might be one of the refreshing *gazpachos* of Andalucía, or a clear broth based on a chicken, meat or seafood broth, garnished with small quantities of the appropriate, more expensive ingredients.

First-course salads are carefully composed mixtures: either dressed, diced, precooked vegetables or fish; or a flat dish of neatly arranged salad ingredients, usually including precooked whole vegetables, and sometimes garnished with hard-boiled eggs and conserved fish. Altogether a more serious undertaking than the plainly-dressed lettuce, onion, tomato and cucumber which refreshes the palate after the main dish.

AJO BLANCO

Iced almond and garlic soup — Serves 4

Preparation time: 20–25 minutes + 1–2 hours chilling

- *2–3 slices of day-old bread, crusts removed, torn into small pieces*
- *75 g (3 oz) blanched almonds*
- *4 garlic cloves*
- *2 tablespoons olive oil*
- *about 900 ml (1½ pints) cold water*
- *2 tablespoons white wine vinegar*
- *a handful of small seedless green grapes*
- *salt*

This is a refreshing cold soup of the peasant bread-soup family, a speciality of Malaga and Granada. The inclusion of almonds is a refinement introduced by the Moors; the grapes are traditional. Make sure your guests like the flavour of raw garlic: it is a wonderful cure for a summer cold.

Put the bread, almonds, garlic, oil and 600 ml (1 pint) of the water into a blender and liquidise thoroughly. This can be done with a pestle and mortar. Add the rest of the water if necessary until you have the consistency you like. Season with salt and vinegar. Leave to infuse in the fridge for an hour or so.

Just before serving, peel the grapes and float them on top of each serving of soup. Don't worry if they sink: it will taste just as good.

SOPA DE MARISCOS AL VINO DE JEREZ

Shellfish soup with sherry — Serves 4

Preparation and cooking time: 20–30 minutes

- *1.2 litres (2 pints) shellfish in the shell or 250 g (8 oz) fresh or canned shelled fish, e.g. mussels, cockles, whelks and clams*
- *50–75 g (2–3 oz) shrimps, peeled if wished*
- *600 ml (1 pint) water*
- *250 ml (8 fl oz) dry sherry or manzanilla*
- *1 onion, sliced finely*
- *1 garlic clove, chopped*
- *2 tablespoons mayonnaise*
- *1 tablespoon lemon juice*
- *1 tablespoon chopped fresh parsley*
- *salt and pepper*

To serve:

- *1 lemon, quartered*

This fisherman's broth is popular round the coast of Cadiz – the port from which Sir Francis Drake captured, in 1587, the Spanish Armada's stock of 2,900 butts of sherry. No wonder the little English frigates won the next round against the galleons.

Scrub the shellfish in clean water, removing the beards and discarding any with damaged shells, or pick them over if they are unshelled. Pick over the shrimps.

Bring the water to the boil with the sherry, onion and garlic. Throw in the shellfish and bring everything back to the boil. If necessary, simmer for 2–3 minutes to allow the shells to open; discard any that do not. Stir in the shrimps. Remove from the heat and stir in the mayonnaise. The soup will turn into a cloudy cream, rather like the Greek *avgolemono*. Add the lemon juice and parsley. Taste and season.

Serve immediately, with lemon quarters and bread. Ice-cold sherry or a salt-tinged *manzanilla* is the proper accompaniment.

SOPA DE CUARTO DE HORA

Fifteen-minute soup — Serves 4

Preparation and cooking time: 15 minutes

- *1.2 litres (2 pints) chicken, meat or vegetable stock, preferably home-made*
- *1½ tablespoons dry sherry or white wine*
- *about 4 tablespoons finely chopped gammon or ham*
- *4 tablespoons cooked rice or a handful of thread noodles*

This is a popular first-course soup which can be quickly prepared with the broth from an old boiling fowl or one-pot stew, or even just a stock cube. 'Sopa Castellana', the version from Castile and around Madrid, adds the egg raw to each portion of boiling broth, so that the egg white just sets in the hot liquid.

Sopa de Cuarto de Hora (Fifteen-minute soup)
Sopa de Mariscos al Vino de Jerez (Shellfish soup with sherry)

2–4 hard-boiled eggs, chopped

4 small sprigs of fresh mint

2 tablespoons chopped fresh parsley

salt and pepper

Bring the stock and sherry or wine to the boil. Stir in the gammon or ham and rice or noodles. Bring back to the boil and cook for a few minutes, enough to soften the noodles if you are using them. Stir in the chopped eggs and bring back to the boil again. Season to taste. Finish with a sprig of mint and a sprinkle of parsley in each bowl.

GAZPACHO

Iced tomato soup (Pictured on front cover and page 8) Serves 4

Preparation time: 25 minutes + 1 hour chilling

1½ slices of day-old bread

300 ml (½ pint) cold water

1 tablespoon wine vinegar

1 garlic clove

½ small or ¼ large cucumber

500 g (1 lb) ripe tomatoes, scalded and skinned

1 green pepper

½ large spanish onion or 1 onion

1 tablespoon olive oil

150 ml (¼ pint) canned tomato juice or water

salt

To garnish (optional):

chopped hard-boiled egg

croûtons fried in olive oil

Gazpacho is a true peasant dish which has become gentrified. At its simplest, and probably most ancient, it is a kind of thick bread porridge flavoured with olive oil, vinegar and garlic (the constant factors), with, if possible, a garnish of green peppers, tomatoes and onions. These days, the most widely appreciated version concentrates more on the vegetable soup aspect than the robust bread porridge, and increasingly leaves out the bread and oil altogether. This special Sunday gazpacho makes a fine compromise.

Put the bread to soak in a few tablespoons of the water with the vinegar and garlic for 10 minutes.

Dice the cucumber and chop the tomatoes roughly. De-seed and chop the green pepper roughly. Chop the onion (leave it out if you need to keep the *gazpacho*, as it ferments rather easily). Put aside a quarter of the chopped vegetables in separate dishes.

Either liquidise the soaked bread and garlic, the rest of the chopped vegetables and the olive oil in a blender, or pound them in a mortar. Add the tomato juice or water and then the rest of the water until you have the consistency you like. Adjust the seasoning with salt. Put the soup in the fridge for an hour at least.

Serve the soup as iced as possible (but do not add ice cubes as they dilute the soup). Hand round the reserved vegetables separately.

Chopped hard-boiled egg and hot bread *croûtons* can be included for a special meal.

ENSALADA DE MARISCOS

Seafood salad — Serves 4

Preparation time: 10–15 minutes + 1 hour marinating

- *5 tablespoons olive oil*
- *2 tablespoons sherry or wine vinegar*
- *250 g (8 oz) mixed cooked fish, e.g. prawns, shrimps, cod flakes, diced monkfish, clams, mussels, cockles and squid*
- *½ green or red pepper, de-seeded and diced*
- *¼ cucumber or 1 pickling cucumber, diced*
- *2–3 spring onions, chopped*
- *1 tablespoon chopped fresh parsley*
- *½ teaspoon coriander seeds, crushed*
- *salt and pepper*

To garnish:

- *a few crisp lettuce leaves*

This is a fine way to transform plainly-cooked leftover fish. In seaside bars it sometimes features octopus or prawns, both luxury fish, but basically anything goes. Make up your own combinations: you are aiming for delicate fishy flavours spiked up with crisp raw vegetables. I sometimes make it with canned tuna and chopped hard-boiled egg.

Whisk the oil and vinegar together and then add the rest of the ingredients. Leave to marinate for an hour or two, or overnight.

Serve with chunks of bread and a few crisp lettuce leaves to decorate.

ENSALADA SEVILLANA

Sevillana salad — Serves 4

Preparation time: 20–25 minutes

- *1 escarole lettuce (frisé or batavia)*
- *4 cooked or canned artichoke hearts and/or 250 g (8 oz) cooked baby green beans*

This is my favourite first course or light summer lunch. It makes the best possible use of Andalucía's fine raw materials: the inclusion of fresh tarragon is unusual, as this is not a herb much featured in the Spanish kitchen.

2 ripe beef tomatoes or 4 tomatoes, chopped roughly

1 tablespoon capers

4 tablespoons green olives stuffed with anchovies

2–3 slices of mild onion

a few fresh tarragon leaves

1 hard-boiled egg

1 garlic clove, chopped

3–4 tablespoons olive oil

2 teaspoons sherry vinegar

198 g (7 oz) can of tuna in oil, drained and flaked roughly

salt

Layer the lettuce, artichoke hearts and/or green beans, tomatoes, capers, olives, onion and tarragon in a shallow dish.

Remove the yolk from the hard-boiled egg and pound with the garlic. Gradually add the oil and then the vinegar. Dress the salad with this piquant cream. Chop the egg white finely and sprinkle over, with the flaked tuna and salt.

ENSALADA ISLAS CANARIAS

Banana and orange salad — Serves 4

Preparation time: 15 minutes

3 oranges

4 large, ripe bananas, sliced

1 tablespoon lemon juice

1 large red pepper, de-seeded and cut into strips

3 tablespoons olive oil

salt and pepper

To finish:

4 tablespoons grated coconut, toasted if not fresh

I made my first trip to the Canary Islands when I was a small girl, on my way to Uruguay with my parents in one of the big liners which crossed the Atlantic to South America. In those post-war days, everyone went by sea, and the Canary Islands were the jumping-off post between the Old World and the southern New. It was in the port of Las Palmas that I saw my first stems of bananas, orange trees and coconut palms. This salad combines those pleasures.

Peel and slice 2 of the oranges and squeeze the juice from the third. Dress the bananas with the lemon juice and toss with the orange slices, orange juice, red pepper, oil, a little salt and plenty of pepper. Divide into bowls and finish with a topping of coconut. Taste the sunshine.

Ensalada Sevillana (Sevillana Salad)
Ensalada Islas Canarias (Banana and orange salad)

EGGS

Eggs are the great strength of the Spanish kitchen and, as befits an agrarian economy with a strong peasant-farming tradition, the surplus provided the pin-money – 'corner-of-the-apron' – for the rural housewife. When I lived in Andalucía, the egg-lady, the *recovera*, still collected surplus eggs from my neighbours, all of whom had a few hens. She would take the eggs for sale to the local market in Algeciras, and her suppliers would receive their payment in kind: salt, sugar, condensed milk and coffee – all items which could not be home-grown or made. These dishes are served either as starters or *tapas*, or as the main dish at midday or after work.

All these recipes require lightly cooked eggs, so current government advice on the safety of our own egg supplies should be taken into account. However, Spanish housewives would not bother to make these dishes at all if they were obliged to cook the eggs rock-hard.

TORTILLA ESPAÑOLA

Spanish potato omelette (Pictured on page 8) — Serves 2 as a main dish or 4 as a starter

Preparation and cooking time: 45 minutes

8 tablespoons olive oil

6 medium-size potatoes, peeled and diced or sliced finely

½ large spanish onion or 1 onion, chopped finely

6 eggs

salt

The Spaniard loves his potato omelette, a thick, juicy egg-cake: this is no French frivolity. Whatever culinary skills she may otherwise lack, every Spanish country girl whips up a beautiful tortilla to serve at any meal. Here also is good provender for the field worker; schoolchildren take a portion for their lunch; toothless old grannies live on it; and it is served as a tapa in every bar from Cadiz to Bilbao.

Heat the oil in a 20 cm (8-inch) omelette or frying pan. Fry the potatoes and onion gently in the oil for about 20 minutes. The vegetables should soften and cook through, but not colour. Transfer the potatoes and onion to a bowl.

Beat the eggs lightly with a little salt and add them to the potato mixture. Pour most of the oil out of the pan, leaving only a tablespoon or two, heat it again and tip in the egg mixture. Fry gently for about 10 minutes until the eggs begin to look set. The heat should be low or the base will burn before the eggs are ready. As it cooks, neaten the sides with a spatula to build up a deep, straight edge. Slide it out onto a plate, then invert it back into the pan and cook the other side for about 5 minutes, A little more oil in the pan may be necessary. Drain well.

Serve warm, cut into neat squares for *tapas*, or quarters if it is to be the centrepiece of the meal. If this is the case, serve a few slices of *serrano* or prosciutto ham and *chorizo* or salami as a starter, and accompany the *tortilla* with the classic Spanish salad of cos lettuce, tomato, cucumber, spanish onion and olives, dressed with olive oil, wine vinegar and salt.

PIPERRADA

Basque eggs — Serves 4 as a starter or 2 as a main dish

Preparation and cooking time: 40 minutes

- *4–5 tablespoons olive oil*
- *1 garlic clove, chopped finely*
- *1 onion, chopped finely*
- *½ aubergine, cubed small*
- *½ green pepper, de-seeded and chopped*
- *½ red pepper, de-seeded and chopped*
- *1 large beef tomato, scalded, skinned and chopped*
- *4 eggs, beaten lightly*
- *salt and pepper*

A rich juicy combination of eggs and vegetables, this Basque speciality is one of the world's great dishes. The vegetables can be prepared ahead, and the eggs scrambled in at the last minute. It is an undemanding recipe, and sometimes includes courgettes, or lacks one or other of the other vegetables. It is good, too, with a bit of ham or chorizo fried in with the garlic.

Heat the oil in a small frying pan. Turn the garlic, onion and aubergine in the hot oil until they soften and take colour. Stir in the peppers and let them soften. Add the tomato and bubble up to make a thick sauce – cook until nearly dry, or the finished dish will be too wet.

Stir in the eggs and scramble them with the vegetables. Remove from the heat as soon as the eggs form curds. Season with salt and pepper. Serve with bread to mop up the juices.

HUEVOS A LA FLAMENCA

Eggs with ham and vegetables

Serves 4 as a starter or 2 as a main dish

Preparation and cooking time: 25–35 minutes

Piperrada (Basque eggs)

4 tablespoons olive oil

1 small onion, chopped

1 garlic clove, chopped

1 tablespoon chopped fresh parsley

50 g (2 oz) serrano ham or lean gammon, cubed

125 g (4 oz) chorizo or other paprika sausage, sliced thickly

Tortilla a la Payesa (Peasant omelette)

This is the dish for 'romerías', the summer pilgrimages to the shrines of the various Virgins, of which the gypsy pilgrimage to Our Lady of the Rocío in the marshland of the Guadalquivir is the most famous. Cooking on the 'romería' is done in a 'cazuela', a shallow earthenware dish which can be balanced over an open fire.

Preheat the oven to Gas Mark 8/230°C/450°F unless using a solid fuel cooker.

Heat the oil in a frying pan. Throw in the onion and garlic. Let them soften and take a little colour. Add the parsley, ham or gammon and

Huevos a la Flamenca
(Eggs with ham and vegetables)

250 g (8 oz) tomatoes, scalded, skinned and chopped roughly
3 tablespoons fresh or frozen green beans, cut into short lengths
3 tablespoons fresh or frozen shelled peas
2–4 eggs
salt and pepper

chorizo or paprika sausage. Fry for a minute and then add the tomatoes. Bubble up to make a thick, aromatic sauce. Stir in the beans and peas and let them stew for 15 minutes if fresh or 5 minutes if defrosted, until soft: they should not be *al dente* for this dish. Season to taste.

Divide the vegetable stew among 2 or 4 small ovenproof dishes or earthenware casseroles. Crack an egg into each dish. Pop them into the oven for about 5 minutes until the egg whites go milky. This can be done on a top heat if you have a solid fuel cooker. Serve immediately – the beauty of the dish is that the eggs are still cooking as you set them on the table, so the yolks can be stirred into the hot vegetables.

TORTILLA A LA PAYESA

Peasant omelette | Serves 2 as a main dish or 4 as a starter

Preparation and cooking time: 40 minutes

3–5 tablespoons olive oil

1 large potato, peeled and diced or sliced finely

50 g (2 oz) salt-cured ham or lean bacon, diced

½ green or red pepper, de-seeded and chopped

1 garlic clove, chopped

1 slice of onion, chopped

50 g (2 oz) fresh or frozen shelled broad beans or peas

1 small tomato, diced

5 eggs

salt and pepper

This is the dish the farmer hopes to find waiting for him when he comes home from the fields. Rural Spanish housewives make it using the local sausage speciality (and these are very variable – their merits fiercely contested) and whatever vegetables are in season.

Heat 3 tablespoons of the oil in a 20 cm (8-inch) omelette or frying pan. Slip in the potato pieces and cook them gently for about 10 minutes until they are quite soft and golden. Remove and put them to drain in a sieve over a bowl to catch the drippings.

Heat the oil again and throw in the ham or bacon, pepper, garlic and onion. Fry gently for 5 minutes until they soften and take colour. Stir in the beans or peas and tomato and bubble up to make a thick sauce.

Beat the eggs lightly with salt and pepper, mix in the potatoes and tip in the contents of the omelette pan. Wipe out the pan. Reheat it with the drippings from the potatoes and the rest of the oil if necessary. Tip in the egg mixture. Cook as a thick pancake, according to the method for Tortilla Española (Spanish potato omelette, page 26).

Serve warm or cool, cut into squares or quarters.

TORTILLA VALENCIANA

Valencian spinach omelette — Serves 2 as a main dish or 4 as a starter

Preparation time: 10–15 minutes + 15 minutes cooking

- *500 g (1 lb) fresh or frozen leaf spinach*
- *4 eggs*
- *1/4–1/2 teaspoon grated nutmeg*
- *1 tablespoon toasted pine kernels or slivered almonds*
- *1–2 tablespoons olive oil*
- *salt and pepper*

Spain has as many varieties of tortilla as housewives to make them. This one is popular in Valencia, which has a large repertoire of vegetable dishes. It is one of my own favourites for a light summer lunch.

Wash the spinach if it is fresh. Remove and discard any tough stalks and shred the leaves. Blanch the spinach in the water which clings to it and drain as soon as it collapses. Cook the spinach according to the packet instructions if it is frozen. Press the spinach dry through a sieve and leave to cool a little.

Lightly beat the eggs with the nutmeg and salt and pepper. Stir in the spinach and the nuts.

Heat the oil in a 20 cm (8-inch) frying or omelette pan. Tip in the egg mixture. Cook as a thick pancake, according to the method for Tortilla Española (Spanish potato omelette, page 26).

Serve warm or cool, cut into squares or quarters, with piping hot chips fried in olive oil and a tomato and mild onion salad.

FISH

Fresh fish from the three seas which lap Spain's long coastline finds its way into every inland market, however tiny the *pueblo* or village. Small fish are usually grilled or fried, the great strength of the Spanish kitchen. Larger fish are often cooked whole in an aromatic broth with vegetables. Basque cooks are particularly strong in this department: one-pot dishes have their origins in the stews prepared by the deep-sea fishermen who operated out of the ports of the Bay of Biscay.

The inshore fisherman's portion is the cheap fish, such as sardines or anchovies, for grilling or conserving, with a handful of the little spiny rockfish which have no commercial value. Spain also has fine freshwater fish: the sparkling mountain streams of Navarra in particular are well-populated with trout. Locals combine the catch with the salt-cured ham which is a speciality of mountain districts.

MEJILLONES EN VINO DE JEREZ

Mussels in sherry — Serves 4 as a starter

Preparation and cooking time: 35 minutes

2.25 litres (4 pints) fresh raw mussels

2 tablespoons olive oil

2 garlic cloves, sliced

4 tablespoons chopped fresh parsley

200 ml (7 fl oz) dry sherry or white wine

Mussels are plentiful in Britain. In Spain, there are at least half a dozen different varieties of 'conchas', bivalves, which are on sale in the markets. They are sometimes cooked 'a la plancha', on a metal sheet laid over a fire to make a simple grill. Shellfish is good for as long as it can hold water in its shell, which it can for a surprisingly long time.

Rinse the shellfish, checking over and discarding any which are broken or gape open.

Put the oil to heat in a wide frying pan or wok. When it is hot, toss in the garlic and fry for a moment. Add the parsley, quickly followed by the shellfish. Pour in the sherry or wine and turn up the heat. Cover with a lid, shaking the pan to redistribute the shells so that all have a chance to cook. If you have no lid, keep moving them with a metal drainer. It will take 3–4 minutes for all the shells to open; discard any that do not. Do not cook them any longer, but serve them immediately. They should not be reheated, but are delicious cold.

PINCHITOS DE RAPE

Monkfish kebabs — Serves 6–8 as a starter or 4 as a main dish

Preparation time: 20 minutes + 1–2 hours marinating + 12–15 minutes cooking

- *500 g (1 lb) filleted monkfish, cubed*
- *1 green pepper, de-seeded and cut into squares*
- *1 onion, cut into squares*
- *1 tablespoon olive oil, plus extra for grilling*
- *1 tablespoon lemon juice*
- *1 garlic clove, chopped*
- *1 teaspoon cumin seeds*
- *1 teaspoon coriander seeds*
- *1 tablespoon finely chopped fresh parsley*
- *salt and pepper*

Monkfish has firm, lobster-like meat which is particularly good grilled. You will need some very thin skewers: in Spain, granny's steel knitting needles are often borrowed for the purpose.

Thread the monkfish, alternating with the green pepper and onion, onto skewers. Combine the oil, lemon juice, garlic, cumin, coriander, parsley and salt and pepper. Paint the kebabs with this aromatic marinade and leave for an hour or two.

Remove the kebabs from the marinade and drain them. Paint them with a little more olive oil and grill fiercely for 12–15 minutes until the edges of the pepper blacken, basting with the marinade.

Pour over the juices and serve with quartered lemons and bread as a first course, or with rice as a main dish.

MARMITA-KUA

Fisherman's hot-pot (Pictured on title page) Serves 4–6 as a main dish

Preparation and cooking time: 1 hour

- *4 cm (1½-inch) thick tuna, bonito, shark or cod steaks weighing 750 g (1½ lb) in total*
- *250 g (8 oz) onions, sliced*
- *2 garlic cloves*
- *1 green or red pepper, deseeded and sliced*
- *500 g (1 lb) tomatoes, scalded, skinned and sliced*
- *1 kg (2 lb) potatoes, peeled and sliced thickly*
- *5 tablespoons olive oil*
- *2 tablespoons chopped fresh parsley*
- *1–2 bay leaves*
- *1.2 litres (2 pints) water*
- *salt and pepper*

This is a speciality of the off-shore fisherman of the Bay of Biscay, a traditional celebration of the first catch of the year. The tuna or bonito is too valuable a catch to be eaten if the fisherman is close enough to market to turn the fish into ready money.

Wipe the fish steaks and season them with salt. Put the rest of the ingredients in a flameproof earthenware casserole or saucepan and bring to the boil. Lay the fish steaks on top, unless using cod, making sure they are submerged. Bring back to the boil, turn the heat right down and leave to simmer very gently, uncovered, for 45 minutes or longer, depending on the thickness of the steaks and potato slices. Baste the fish frequently. If you are using cod, add it after 15 minutes.

If necessary, remove the fish and allow the sauce to bubble up and reduce. Don't worry if the onions and potatoes at the bottom have stuck to the pan and browned a little: it will be all the more delicious. Leftovers make a lovely hash – *ropa vieja*, 'old clothes'.

CABALLA EN ESCABECHE

Spiced mackerel — Serves 4 as a starter or 2 as a main dish

Preparation and cooking time: 45 minutes + overnight marinating

- *500 g (1 lb) whole, cleaned mackerel*
- *1 heaped tablespoon plain flour*
- *2 tablespoons olive oil*
- *1 small onion, chopped*
- *1 garlic clove, chopped*
- *1 small carrot, chopped*
- *1 tablespoon chopped fresh parsley*
- *1 teaspoon chopped fresh or dried oregano*
- *1 bay leaf*
- *4 crushed peppercorns*
- *1 teaspoon chilli powder (cayenne)*
- *4 tablespoons sherry or wine vinegar*
- *2 tablespoons water*
- *salt*

Mackerel shoals in very large numbers, so the inshore fishing fleet often comes back to port with more fish than the inhabitants can possibly consume fresh. So in the old days, spicy pickle-baths were a way not only to conserve the catch for a few extra days, but also to add variety to the diet. The pickle is good with any leftover fish.

Behead and wipe the mackerel. Chop it straight through the bone to give 4–5 thick steaks. Sprinkle the slices with salt and dust them with the flour. Heat the oil in a shallow frying pan until it is hot. Slip in the fish steaks and fry them golden (don't let them overcook, they should be firm). Transfer the cooked fish to a shallow dish.

Fry the onion and garlic gently in the oil which remains in the pan, adding extra if necessary, until softened. Add the carrot, parsley, oregano, bay leaf and peppercorns. Fry the aromatics gently for a few moments to allow the flavours to mingle. Sprinkle in the chilli powder and a little salt, pour in the sherry or wine vinegar and water and allow the mixture to bubble up. Scrape in all the little sticky bits in the pan.

Pour this warm, scented bath unstrained over the fish. Cover loosely with a clean cloth or clingfilm and leave at least overnight in a cool place or in the fridge for the aromatics to penetrate and pickle the fish. It is ready to eat in a day, better in two, and will keep for a week in the fridge.

CHANGURRO

Basque crab

Serves 4 as a starter

Preparation and cooking time: 25–30 minutes (+ 20–25 minutes if using whole crab)

250 g (8 oz) dressed crab meat, preferably in the shell

3 tablespoons olive oil

Trucha a la Navarra (Baked trout with ham and red wine)

50 g (2 oz) butter

1 small leek, chopped

1 small onion, chopped

1 garlic clove, chopped

1 teaspoon paprika

¼ teaspoon chilli powder (cayenne)

1 teaspoon tomato purée

125 ml (4 fl oz) dry sherry, white wine or cider

1 tablespoon brandy or Calvados (optional)

1 tablespoon chopped fresh parsley

1–2 tablespoons fresh breadcrumbs

salt and pepper

This is the classic Basque way with the clawless, long-legged spider-crabs – 'centollas' – which are harvested off the coast of Guipuzcoa. It is a particularly delicious recipe, and can be made with any variety of crab meat, white and dark together, even canned.

Pick over the crab meat and remove any bits of shell.

Warm the oil with half the butter and sprinkle in the leek, onion and garlic. Let the vegetables soften. Stir in the crab meat and let it bubble up. Stir in the paprika, chilli powder, tomato purée, sherry, wine or cider and brandy or Calvados, if used, and let it boil fiercely for a minute to evaporate the alcohol. Taste and add salt and

Caballa en Escabeche
(Spiced mackerel)

Changurro
(Basque crab)

pepper. Return the crab mixture to the shell or a small shallow casserole. At this point the crab can be left for later reheating, or even frozen as it is.

To finish, sprinkle with the parsley and breadcrumbs, dot with the remaining butter and grill for a few minutes until the top is brown and bubbling. (If reheating, heat through gently in the oven before gilding under the grill.)

Serve with chunks of bread to mop up the juices. It is also good served with rice if you prefer.

TRUCHA A LA NAVARRA

Baked trout with ham and red wine — Serves 4

Preparation time: 20 minutes + 1–2 hours marinating + 15–20 minutes cooking

- *4 whole trout, cleaned*
- *2 slices of serrano or Parma ham or gammon, chopped*
- *a few fresh mint leaves*
- *1 spring onion, chopped very finely*
- *1 teaspoon chopped fresh or dried thyme*
- *1 bay leaf*
- *175 ml (6 fl oz) red wine*
- *4 tablespoons olive oil*
- *1 egg, whisked lightly*
- *salt and pepper*

This dish from the mountains of Navarra combines the hill-people's two favourite pleasures – trout from the upland streams, and the wind-dried salted ham which can only be prepared in the dry, cold climate of Spain's mountain ranges.

Stuff the cavities of the trout with the ham or gammon and mint leaves. Lay the fish in a flameproof casserole which will just accommodate them. Sprinkle with the spring onion and thyme, tuck in the bay leaf and pour in the red wine. Cover and leave to marinate for an hour or two.

Bring to the boil, pour in the oil and add a little salt and pepper. Cover and simmer for 15–20 minutes. Remove the trout and take the sauce off the heat. Whisk 1 tablespoon of the hot sauce into the egg and then add to the rest of the sauce; do not reheat.

Serve the trout with plain-boiled potatoes, with the sauce poured round.

PEZ ESPADA O ATÚN EN ESCABECHE A LA PLANCHA

Griddled marinated swordfish or tuna steaks — Serves 3–4 as a main dish

Preparation time: 20 minutes + 3 hours marinating + 5 minutes cooking

- *4 thin-cut tuna or swordfish steaks, or halibut, cod, haddock or salmon, weighing 500 g (1 lb) in total*
- *2 tablespoons olive oil, plus extra for frying*
- *juice of 1 lemon*

Large fish such as swordfish and tuna are easier to keep fresh than small fish. Much prized as a luxury dish, the fish is given the same treatment as meat: sliced in thin steaks and grilled. In this delicious recipe, the fish is marinated with herbs and spices to give it extra flavour.

2 garlic cloves, chopped

1 tablespoon chopped fresh parsley

1 tablespoon paprika

½ teaspoon crushed peppercorns

1 teaspoon chopped fresh oregano

1 teaspoon salt

To serve:

lemon quarters

Wipe the fish steaks. Mix together the rest of the ingredients to make a marinade and place in a shallow dish. Lay in the fish, cover and leave to marinate for a few hours or overnight, turning the steaks once or twice.

Lay the fillets on a very hot griddle or a heavy frying pan brushed with oil. Let the steaks take the heat first on one side and then on the other. The time needed is in proportion to the thickness of the steaks, but 2–3 minutes on each side just to brown should be enough. Serve immediately, with lemon quarters and thick-cut crisp chips.

BOQUERONES FRITOS

Little fried fish — Serves 4–5 as a starter

Preparation and cooking time: 25–30 minutes

500 g (1 lb) fresh small sardines, sprats, anchovies or large whitebait

4 heaped tablespoons strong unbleached plain flour

1 heaped teaspoon salt

oil for frying, e.g. olive and sunflower

To serve:

lemon quarters

The housewives of Spain seem to have the knack of frying fish to perfection. Put it down to the superb raw materials available, and the beautiful olive oil, good rough salt and well-tempered iron pans.

Rinse and, if necessary, scale and gut the fish by running your finger down their soft bellies (see page 14). Remove the heads if you wish. Sieve the flour onto a flat plate and mix in the salt. Using damp fingers, pinch the tails of the fish together in fans of 3 to 5, depending on size. Dust them through the flour, pressing the tails firmly together to make little fish fans.

Heat about 1 cm (½ inch) of oil in a shallow frying pan. When the oil is hot, lay in the fish head-first, only 2 or 3 fans at a time, or the temperature drops too fast. Fry the fish until crisp and golden, turning them half-way through. Remove them with a draining spoon and transfer to kitchen paper to blot up the oil. Serve straight away, accompanied by quarters of lemon.

GAMBAS PIL-PIL

Prawns with garlic and chilli — Serves 4 as a starter

Preparation and cooking time: 10–15 minutes

375 g (12 oz) peeled small prawns, preferably raw

8–10 tablespoons olive oil

1–2 garlic cloves, slivered

1 small dried red chilli pepper, de-seeded and chopped, or ¼ teaspoon chilli powder (cayenne)

salt

This dish is also known as 'gambas al ajillo' – garlic prawns. I am told by the Valencians that the name 'pil-pil' is onomatopoeic and comes from the bubbling of the oily juices. However, I prefer the explanation offered in my local seaport in Andalucía: that it is a relic of the Moorish occupation. Crab is also excellent prepared this way, but it needs a splash of sherry or brandy to keep it moist.

Pick over the prawns and remove any stray whiskers.

Heat the oil in 2 small shallow casseroles over a high heat. When the oil is sizzling, carefully add the garlic and a little salt. Let it take a little colour, then carefully drop in the prawns and chilli. Stir the prawns quickly, adding more oil if it is all absorbed. Serve the prawns immediately in the cooking dish, with bread for mopping up the delicious aromatic oil.

Boquerones Fritos (Little fried fish)
Gambas Pil-Pil (Prawns with garlic and chilli)

VEGETABLES

The recipes in this section are all suitable for vegetarians: in fact most of Spain's large repertoire of vegetable and pulse dishes are easy to convert to the demands of non-meat eaters. Vegetables in Spain are often served as a first course, so all that is usually necessary is to leave out a tiny quantity of ham, used almost like a stock cube in Spain. Three or four 'starter' dishes will make a main course.

Spain specialises, naturally enough, in those Mediterranean vegetables which need plenty of sunshine. Nevertheless, all the familiar northern vegetables grow very well in the fertile climate. Less familiar vegetables in the markets include a wide variety of wild greens. Mushrooms most commonly available are the familiar cultivated variety. It is really only the inhabitants of the north and east who appreciate their wild fungi, with most attention paid to the autumn crop of saffron milkcaps: bright orange fungi which bruise blue.

PIMENTOS RELLENOS CON ARROZ Y ALMENDRAS

Peppers stuffed with rice and almonds

Serves 4 as a starter or 2 as a main dish

Preparation time: 40 minutes + ¾–1¼ hours cooking

- *4 large or 5–6 medium-size red or green peppers*
- *6 saffron threads or ½ teaspoon turmeric*
- *4 tablespoons olive oil*
- *2 garlic cloves, chopped*
- *50 g (2 oz) flaked or halved almonds*
- *1 tablespoon paprika*
- *1 tablespoon chopped fresh parsley*
- *500 g (1 lb) tomatoes, scalded, skinned and chopped, or a 397 g (14 oz) can of chopped tomatoes*
- *150 ml (¼ pint) water*
- *250 g (8 oz) Italian or risotto rice*
- *½ teaspoon salt*

This is a recipe from Alcoy in the hills behind Valencia. Almonds, saffron and rice are characteristically Moorish ingredients – the orange groves of Valencia are still watered by the Moors' irrigation systems.

Preheat the oven to Gas Mark 7/220°C/425°F.

Cut a lid off each pepper round the stalk end, leaving the stalk in place. Scoop out the seeds. If using saffron, leave it to infuse in a splash of hot water and then crush.

Heat the oil gently in a frying pan, scatter in the garlic and almonds and fry for a few moments, until the almonds have taken a little colour and the garlic has softened. Stir in the paprika, parsley, tomatoes and water and bubble up. Sprinkle in the rice. Add the salt and crushed saffron or turmeric and remove from the heat.

Stuff the peppers with the rice – they should be only half full as the rice needs room to swell. Arrange the peppers upright in a pan which will just accommodate them. Replace their lids. Cover and cook in the oven for ¾–1¼ hours, depending on the size of the peppers. You may need to reduce the temperature during cooking. Test the rice by biting a grain: the rice on top should be very soft or the middle will be too hard.

Serve the peppers with the juices, hot or cool: they are nicest at room temperature.

PISTO MANCHEGO

Vegetable hot-pot

Serves 4–6 as a main dish or 10 as a starter

Preparation and cooking time: about 1½ hours

6 tablespoons olive oil

1 large spanish onion, chopped

3 garlic cloves, chopped

1 red and/or 1 green pepper, de-seeded and sliced lengthways

1–2 tablespoons chopped serrano ham or gammon (optional)

1 small green chilli, de-seeded and chopped finely (optional)

1–2 bay leaves

500 g (1 lb) ripe tomatoes, scalded, skinned and chopped, or a 397 g (14 oz) can of chopped tomatoes

This rich vegetable stew comes from Don Quixote's home territory, La Mancha, Spain's high, dry, red-earthed central plateau. I had my first taste of a pisto many years ago in a little bar in the ramparts of Toledo, the medieval walled city of swordmakers. My portion, served in its own little round earthenware dish, came topped with a fried egg – cooked, Spanish-style, in very hot shallow olive oil, so that the edges of the white were a crispy golden lace and the yolk still runny. Pisto has been a favourite family supper dish ever since.

Heat the olive oil in a deep frying pan. Add the onion and garlic and fry gently until they take a little colour. Add the pepper(s) and ham or

Coca Alicantina (Pizza-bread with tomatoes and peppers)

150 ml (¼ pint) red wine

6–7 young carrots, sliced

1 kg (2 lb) potatoes, peeled and sliced thickly

250 g (8 oz) green beans

2–3 courgettes, sliced

salt and pepper

To finish:

2 tablespoons finely chopped fresh parsley

1 tablespoon finely chopped fresh marjoram

1 garlic clove, chopped finely (optional)

gammon and chilli, if used. Tuck in the bay leaf or leaves. Fry gently to soften and take a little colour. Add the tomatoes and leave to simmer quietly, uncovered, to a thick purée.

Pour in the wine and bring to the boil. Add the carrots and potatoes and enough water to almost submerge all the vegetables. Turn down the heat, cover and leave to simmer for 15 minutes. Test the potatoes and carrots with a fork. When they are almost soft, lay in the beans and courgettes. Season to taste, cover and cook for another 5 minutes.

To finish, take off the lid, turn up the heat and let the sauce bubble fiercely for a few minutes to evaporate extra moisture and thicken the sauce. Sprinkle in the parsley and marjoram right at the end, so that their flavour remains fresh, and add the garlic, if used.

Serve the aromatic vegetable stew either as a starter, or on its own as a light supper dish, in which case top each portion with an egg, either fried or hard-boiled and quartered.

Pimentos Rellenos con Arroz y Almendras (Peppers stuffed with rice and almonds)

Pisto Manchego (Vegetable hot-pot)

COCA ALICANTINA

Pizza-bread with tomatoes and peppers — Serves 2–4

Preparation time: 1 hour + 25–30 minutes baking

For the topping:

4 tablespoons olive oil, plus extra for sprinkling

1 garlic clove, chopped

1 small onion, sliced finely

1 small green or red pepper, de-seeded and cut into strips

2 beef tomatoes, scalded, skinned and chopped, or a 397 g (14 oz) can of chopped tomatoes

125 g (4 oz) fresh or frozen leaf spinach, blanched or defrosted and chopped roughly

½ teaspoon grated nutmeg

salt and pepper

For the base:

150 ml (¼ pint) water

10–12 tablespoons olive oil, plus extra for greasing

1 teaspoon salt

300 g (10 oz) unbleached plain flour, sieved, plus extra for rolling

To finish:

2 tablespoons fresh breadcrumbs, fried crisp in olive oil

The coca is a flat bread much like the Middle Eastern pitta. It is a speciality of Spain's eastern seaboard. It is certainly a bread of ancient pedigree: country people will tell you that it should ideally be cooked on the raked embers of a camp-fire. More sophisticated cocas are raised with yeast; I give a primitive unleavened form here. As with pizza, you can vary the topping as you please. If you are in a hurry, sliced bread sprinkled with oil will do as the base.

Preheat the oven to Gas Mark 6/200°C/400°F. Alternatively, the *coca* can be cooked on a griddle.

Prepare the topping. Heat the olive oil in a small frying pan. Add the garlic and onion and fry gently until they soften. Add the pepper and fry until the vegetables take a little colour. Stir in the tomatoes, spinach and nutmeg and bubble up for 25 minutes to make a rich, thick jam. Season to taste.

Meanwhile, pour the water, 6 tablespoons of the oil and the salt into a bowl. Work in enough flour to give a soft dough and knead it until smooth. Roll the dough out on a floured board. Sprinkle with some of the remaining oil and fold over itself. Roll out again and repeat the operation another 3 times, adding more of the oil each time. The final time, roll the dough into a 30 cm (12-inch) round. Oil a baking tin and lay in the dough. Knuckle the centre towards the edges a little to give you a rim which will contain the juicy topping.

Spread the topping over the *coca*. Sprinkle with a little more oil. Bake near the top of the oven for 25–30 minutes, until the *coca* is nicely crisped. Finish with a sprinkling of fried breadcrumbs and serve immediately. To serve it as a main course, sprinkle with grated cheese 10 minutes before the end of baking.

HABAS A LA RONDEÑA

Broad bean hot-pot — Serves 6 as a starter or 3–4 as a main dish

Preparation time: 20 minutes + 1–1½ hours cooking

1 kg (2 lb) young broad beans in their pods

a small bunch of fresh parsley

1 bay leaf

a sprig of fresh thyme

150 ml (¼ pint) olive oil

1 onion, chopped

3 garlic cloves, chopped

1–2 tablespoons chopped serrano ham or gammon (optional)

4 tablespoons dry sherry or white wine

300 ml (½ pint) water

1 teaspoon sugar

salt and pepper

To finish:

1–2 tablespoons fresh breadcrumbs

1 tablespoon finely chopped fresh parsley

1 tablespoon finely chopped fresh marjoram

½ tablespoon grated lemon zest

This stew, one of my favourite Spanish dishes, is at its best made when the broad beans are small and tender and the pods, not yet stringy and tough, can be included. The slightly sticky, velvety texture of the pods is not unlike okra. The stew can of course be made with older, podded beans (in which case some cooks add the scraped-off fluff from the pod). These last can be frozen, or dried ('ful') and presoaked.

Top, tail and string the beans and chop them into short lengths, more or less following the swell of each bean. Do not do this ahead of time or the beans will go an odd navy-blue colour at the edges. Tie the parsley, bay leaf and thyme into a little bunch.

Heat the oil in a large pan. Put in the onion and garlic and fry for a moment without allowing them to take colour. Add the beans, bunch of herbs, ham or gammon, if used, sherry or wine and water. Bring to the boil, reduce the heat, cover and stew gently for 1–1½ hours, checking and adding extra water if necessary. Add salt and pepper and a little sugar when the beans are tender.

Turn up the heat and cook the stew, uncovered, for a moment to evaporate all but a rich slick of oily juice. Remove the bunch of herbs and then stir in the breadcrumbs, herbs and lemon zest. Top each portion with a quartered hard-boiled egg if serving as a main dish.

This juicy aromatic stew is lovely with thick slices of bread, grilled, rubbed with garlic and trickled with olive oil. Any leftovers, drained of extra juices, make a fine *tortilla*, as in the recipe for Tortilla Valenciana (Valencian spinach omelette, page 31).

MACHACÓN

Potatoes with pepper and tomato — Serves 2–4

Preparation time: 20 minutes + 1–1½ hours cooking

- *4 large baking potatoes*
- *2 tablespoons pine kernels or slivered almonds*
- *1 teaspoon cumin seeds*
- *3–6 tablespoons olive oil*
- *1 green pepper, de-seeded and chopped finely*
- *1 red pepper, de-seeded and chopped finely*
- *1 large tomato, scalded, skinned and chopped finely*
- *¼ cucumber, chopped finely*
- *grated zest and juice of 1 lemon*
- *salt and pepper*

This cheap-and-cheerful dish from La Mancha is made with baking potatoes in the winter: the winters in these uplands are hard, and a baked potato is comforting. It is made with new potatoes in the spring, and potatoes plain-boiled and sliced in the summer.

Preheat the oven to Gas Mark 6/200°C/400°F.

Scrub and bake the potatoes for 1–1½ hours, depending on size, until they are soft.

Fry the nuts and cumin seeds quickly in a tablespoon of the oil. Mix the contents of the frying pan with the chopped vegetables. Fold in the lemon juice and zest and the rest of the oil, and add salt and pepper to taste.

Split the baked potatoes and stuff them with the vegetable mixture: lovely on a cold day. If you use boiled potatoes, turn them in the sauce.

CALABACINES Y BEREGENAS FRITOS CON SALSA DE TOMATE

Courgette and aubergine fritters with tomato sauce — Serves 4

Preparation time: 15 minutes + 30 minutes salting + 15–20 minutes cooking

For the fritters:

- *500 g (1 lb) courgettes*
- *1 large, firm aubergine*
- *50 ml (2 fl oz) milk*
- *6 tablespoons unbleached plain flour*
- *oil for frying*
- *salt and pepper*

Simple and delicious, these crisp mouthfuls make a lovely entrée to a meal. For a main course for two, replace some of the milk with a lightly beaten egg and serve grated cheese as well as the tomato sauce. In my family the fritters vanish as soon as they come out of the pan.

Machacón (Potatoes with pepper and tomato)
Calabacines y Beregenas Fritos con Salsa de Tomate (Courgette and aubergine fritters with tomato sauce)

For the sauce:

500 g (1 lb) tomatoes, scalded, skinned and chopped, or a 397 g (14 oz) can of chopped tomatoes

2 tablespoons olive oil

1 green chilli, de-seeded and chopped (optional)

1 garlic clove, chopped

½ onion, chopped

Cut the courgettes and aubergine into thin slices lengthways. Salt the slices and put them in a colander to drain for half an hour (I don't always do this, but it does help draw out the bitter juices). Rinse and pat dry.

Put all the ingredients for the sauce in a liquidiser and process them to a purée. Put the purée into a small pan and let it bubble gently on a low heat while you make the fritters.

Pour the milk onto a flat plate. Spread the flour on another plate. Season it with salt and pepper. Heat 2.5 cm (1 inch) of oil in a frying pan. When it is hot, dip the slices of courgette and aubergine first in the milk and then in the flour. Slip them into the hot oil, a few at a time, and fry them crisp. Transfer to kitchen paper to drain. Continue until all the slices are done.

Serve the fritters immediately, with the sauce served separately.

SETAS AL HORNO

Baked mushrooms with parsley and garlic — Serves 4

Preparation time: 15–20 minutes + 20–25 minutes cooking

375 g (12 oz) mushrooms

125 ml (4 fl oz) sherry, plus extra if necessary

4–5 tablespoons olive oil

2 garlic cloves, chopped finely

2 heaped tablespoons chopped fresh parsley

2 heaped tablespoons fresh breadcrumbs

salt and pepper

Bright orange saffron milk caps are used for this in Valencia. Further north, where the French influence is strong, a wide variety of wild fungi is gathered. In Andalucía, big flat field mushrooms are gathered by the gypsies and offered for sale in the markets in the autumn. The drier the mushroom, the more sherry and oil they can absorb. Try the recipe with oyster mushrooms or shiitake. To convert it into a main course for two, finish with grated cheese as well as breadcrumbs.

Preheat the oven to Gas Mark 6/200°C/400°F.

Wipe the mushrooms but do not peel them. Trim the stalks level with the caps, reserving the trimmings, and arrange them in a shallow ovenproof dish which will just accommodate them. Tuck the stalk trimmings in the gaps. Trickle the sherry and olive oil over. Season with salt and pepper. Bake in the oven, uncovered, for 10 minutes, basting frequently. Add more sherry if necessary.

Toss the garlic, parsley and breadcrumbs lightly together. Sprinkle over the mushrooms and baste with the mushroom juices. Return the dish to the oven for 10–15 minutes, basting as necessary.

Serve the mushrooms sizzling hot in their cooking dish: it would be a shame to waste those delicious juices.

ALCACHOFAS ESTOFADAS CON PIÑONES

Baked artichokes with pine kernels — Serves 4–6

Preparation time: 30 minutes + 25–30 minutes cooking

6–12 globe artichokes, depending on size

grated zest and juice of 1 lemon, plus extra for boiling

4 tablespoons olive oil

500 g (1 lb) onions, sliced finely

4 garlic cloves, chopped

250 ml (8 fl oz) white wine

300 ml (½ pint) water

salt and pepper

To finish:

1 tablespoon pine kernels or slivered almonds, toasted

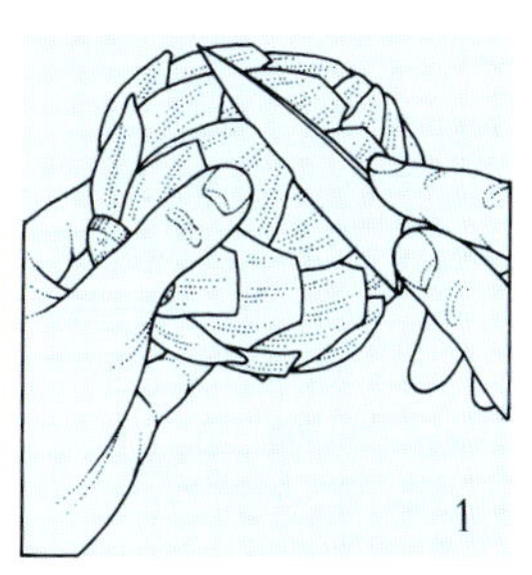

1

Granada has the best artichokes in Spain, a legacy of the Moors, whose irrigated gardens were their pride and joy. There are many varieties of artichoke in Spain and many ways of preparing them. This extravagant recipe is my favourite: it should be saved for mid-season when artichokes are cheap, as it uses only the plump, juicy hearts. For a main course for two or three, add a dish of plainly-cooked potatoes dressed with olive oil, lemon juice and chopped onion.

Prepare the artichokes. Trim off the stem of each one (if it is tender, scrape it and include it, chopped into short lengths, with the rest of the flesh). Break off the larger outside leaves. Trim off the rest of the leaves, leaving only the tender lower edges attached to the base and a cone of inner leaves (1). With a very sharp knife, trim the remaining leaves straight across the choke (2). Continue until all the artichokes are ready.

Preheat the oven to Gas Mark 6/200°C/400°F.

Bring a pan of salted water with a dash of lemon juice to the boil. Slip in the artichoke hearts and blanch them for 5–8 minutes. Drain them and then scoop out the chokes with a firm twist of a sharp teaspoon (3). If the artichokes are small, leave them whole; if large, quarter them. Arrange them in a single layer in an ovenproof dish.

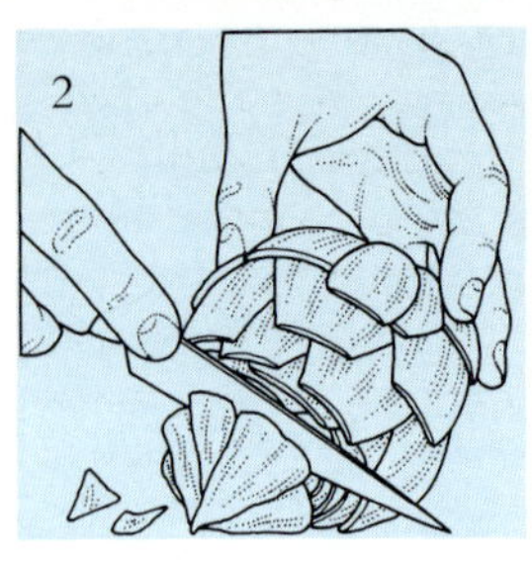

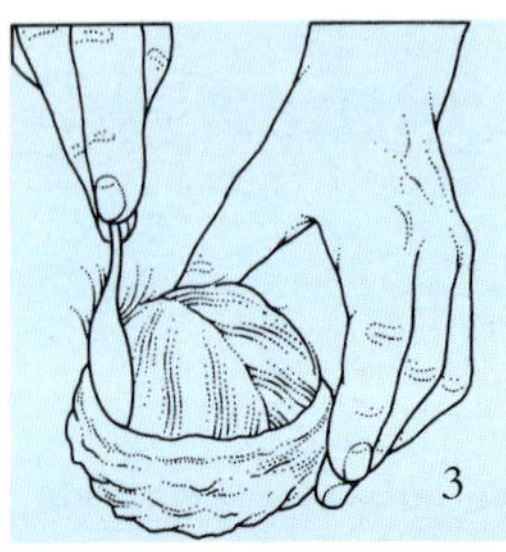

Meanwhile, heat the oil in a frying pan and gently fry the onions and garlic until they soften and gild. Pour in the wine and water and bubble up. Add salt and pepper and the lemon juice and zest.

Pour the hot aromatic bath over the artichokes. Cover and transfer to the oven. Bake for 25–30 minutes until the artichokes are tender. Let them cool and re-absorb some of the juices. Sprinkle with the toasted pine kernels or slivered almonds just before serving. Serve warm or at room temperature.

PEZ DE TIERRA

Aubergine purée — Serves 4

Preparation and cooking time: 30 minutes

150 ml (¼ pint) olive oil

3 garlic cloves, chopped roughly

2 large, firm aubergines, cut into 2.5 cm (1-inch) dice

1 teaspoon ground cumin

1 teaspoon ground coriander

2 tablespoons chopped fresh parsley

grated zest and juice of 1 lemon

1–2 tablespoons fresh breadcrumbs

salt and pepper

This spicy purée – literally translated it means 'earth fish' – is a speciality of the Levante, the eastern region. Variations of it appear all round the Mediterranean, where good Catholics in medieval times observed more than half the year as meatless fast days. The ingredients were considerably cheaper than 'pez de monte' or 'mountain fish' – the nickname given to salt cod, the alternative fasting-food. To serve as a main dish for two, finish with quartered hard-boiled eggs.

Heat the oil in a large, shallow pan. Add the garlic and cook it for a minute or two. Add the aubergine. Fry, turning as each side cooks, for about 10 minutes on a medium heat, until the aubergine is soft and just lightly browned.

Pour the contents of the pan into a food processor with the spices, parsley and lemon juice and zest, and reduce it all to a speckled purée. This can also be done with a pestle and mortar, which will give a denser, richer texture. Stir in the breadcrumbs to mop up any unabsorbed oil, and season to taste.

Serve the purée at room temperature, with crisp lettuce leaves and hunks of bread for dipping.

ESPINACAS A LA CATALANA

Spinach with almonds and raisins — Serves 4

Preparation and cooking time: 15–25 minutes

500 g (1 lb) fresh or frozen leaf spinach or chard leaves

2 tablespoons raisins or sultanas

grated zest and juice of 1 orange

2 tablespoons slivered almonds or pine kernels

4–5 tablespoons olive oil

½ teaspoon grated nutmeg

½ teaspoon ground cinnamon

salt and pepper

To finish:

lemon juice or wine vinegar

This dish has the flavours of Morocco – not surprising since the Moors were in Spain for several centuries, quite long enough to pass on their culinary habits to the natives. The raisins and nuts and spices are lovely Levantine flavourings. To serve as a main dish for two, finish with quartered hard-boiled eggs: it is a little light on its own.

If using fresh spinach or chard, rinse, pick over, shred and cook in a covered pan with a little salt and the minimum of water. This will take about 5 minutes only. Cook frozen leaf spinach according to the packet instructions.

Meanwhile, put the raisins or sultanas to plump in the orange juice. Fry the nuts golden in the olive oil and then stir in the spices, off the heat.

Drain the spinach well in a sieve and turn it in the hot oil with the nuts and spices, raisins or sultanas and grated orange zest. Season to taste. Reheat and finish with a sprinkle of lemon juice or wine vinegar.

RICE

The rice dishes of Spain are closer in spirit to the juicy risottos of Italy than they are to the dry-cooked rice of the East. They are traditionally only served at midday. Saffron is almost always included and the flavouring ingredients are either cooked in the broth and served first, or served together with the rice. Any Valencian housewife worth her paella pan can probably come up with fifty different combinations for flavouring the basic saffron rice. I give my version, but feel free to make your own contribution. I would not be so foolish as to attempt to define the true Valencian *paella*, a matter over which families are wrenched apart and strong men come to blows.

MOROS Y CRISTIANOS

Black beans and white rice — Serves 4

Preparation time: overnight soaking + 30–40 minutes + 2 hours cooking

For the beans:

300 g (10 oz) black or pinto beans, soaked overnight

125 g (4 oz) streaky bacon, diced

1 bay leaf

2 tablespoons olive oil

1 onion, chopped

1 garlic clove, chopped

2 heaped tablespoons chopped fresh parsley

1 tablespoon paprika

1 tomato, scalded, skinned and chopped

salt and pepper

This delightfully-named dish of white rice and black beans commemorates Christian deliverance from the Moorish occupation of Spain. Many small 'pueblos' or villages have 'ferias' – carnivals – which mark local battles with the Moors, often featuring a full-scale mock battle in the narrow whitewashed streets. This is the dish with which victory is celebrated.

Drain the beans and bring them to the boil in enough water to cover them to a depth of 2.5 cm (1 inch). Add the bacon and bay leaf, turn down the heat, cover and leave to bubble gently for 1½–2 hours until the beans are soft. Add more boiling water as necessary, but not too much: you want the beans to end up almost cooked dry. Drain off any excess at the end if necessary and remove the bay leaf.

Preheat the oven to Gas Mark 2/150°C/300°F. Butter a 900 ml (1½-pint) ring mould.

Meanwhile, about 30 minutes before the

For the rice:

900 ml (1½ pints) chicken stock, or a mixture of water and white wine

375 g (12 oz) Italian or risotto rice

40 g (1½ oz) lard or butter, softened, plus extra for greasing

1 teaspoon grated lemon zest

½ teaspoon grated nutmeg

4 tablespoons grated cheese, e.g. Manchego, Cheddar or parmesan

1 egg, forked roughly

salt and pepper

beans finish cooking, prepare the rice. Bring the stock or water-and-wine to the boil and shower in the rice. Add salt if using the water-and-wine. Bring back to the boil, cover and leave to cook for about 20 minutes until the rice is soft and the liquid is all absorbed. Season to taste. Remove from the heat and beat in the lard or butter, lemon zest, nutmeg, cheese, and – finally – the egg. Pack the rice into the mould and cover with greased foil. Alternatively, mould the rice by hand or pack it into little cocotte dishes. Put to warm in the oven for 10 minutes.

While the rice is warming, make a traditional Valencian *sofrito* for the beans. Heat the oil and throw in the onion, garlic, parsley and paprika. Fry gently for a few minutes, then turn up the heat and stir in the tomato. Let it bubble up into a rich little sauce. Stir the sauce into the beans. Taste and add salt and pepper.

Unmould the rice onto a large round plate or make a ring round the edge of the plate. Fill the middle with the black beans, either in neat little moulded piles, or heaped up.

The battle is won: you have the Moors surrounded by the Christians. Toast the victory in anis-flavoured white brandy – *aguardiente*.

ARROZ A BANDA

Two-dish rice ('Rice apart') Serves 6–8

Preparation and cooking time: about 1 hour

- *2–3 garlic cloves*
- *2 tablespoons paprika, or 2 dried red peppers (ñoras), fried*
- *10–12 saffron threads or 1 teaspoon yellow colouring*
- *1.2 litres (2 pints) water*
- *a sprig of fresh thyme*
- *1 bay leaf*
- *150 ml (¼ pint) white wine*
- *8 tablespoons olive oil*
- *1 kg (2 lb) mixed fish cutlets or steaks, e.g. lobster, tuna, swordfish, cod, haddock, sole, plaice and squid rings*
- *a few large raw prawns or freshwater crayfish and fresh raw mussels or clams (optional)*
- *2 tablespoons chopped fresh parsley*
- *500 g (1 lb) tomatoes, scalded, skinned and chopped*
- *500–600 g (1–1¼ lb) Italian or risotto rice*
- *salt and pepper*

For the al i olli:

- *6 garlic cloves*
- *1 teaspoon salt*
- *300 ml (½ pint) virgin olive oil*

Arroz a Banda (Two-dish rice)

This is the second and least known of the two great rice dishes of Valencia. It has its name because the fish is served while the rice is cooking, and it is this presentation of two courses which differentiates it from a paella. The fish is served with 'al i olli', a punchy little sauce of garlic and oil, or a well-garlicked mayonnaise.

Make the *al i olli* first. Pound the garlic in a mortar with the salt. Slowly trickle in the oil, working the paste so that the garlic acts as an emulsifier to make a rich, spoonable sauce. If you are in a hurry, make it in a liquidiser with a peeled, boiled potato, or a crust of stale bread, soaked and squeezed, to stabilise it. Those uncertain of good results can make it with an egg yolk, like a garlic mayonnaise, which gives a richer but less piquant mix.

For the rice: pound the garlic in another mortar with the paprika or peppers and a teaspoon of salt and set aside. If using saffron, leave to infuse in a splash of boiling water and then crush.

Heat the water in a large pan with the thyme, bay leaf, wine and 4 tablespoons of the oil. Season and add the firm-fleshed fish (lobster, tuna, swordfish, squid). Bring to the boil, turn down the heat and leave to simmer for 8 minutes. Add the soft-fleshed fish (cod, haddock, sole, plaice) and shellfish and crustaceans, if used, and leave to simmer for 8 minutes more. Carefully lift out the fish and pile it in a serving dish to keep warm (this is served while the rice cooks). Measure and reserve the fish stock – you will need just over 1 litre (1¾ pints). Boil it to reduce and concentrate the flavours if necessary.

Heat the rest of the oil in a wide frying or *paella* pan. Add the parsley, tomatoes, crushed garlic and paprika or peppers, and saffron or

colouring. Stir in the rice and pour in double the volume of fish stock to the volume of rice. Bring to the boil and bubble fiercely for 5 minutes, then turn down the heat and simmer for another 12 minutes. Trickle in more fish stock as necessary. Remove from the heat and leave to rest for 10–15 minutes. The rice should be juicy but the grains separate.

While the rice is cooking, serve the fish with the *al i olli*. By the time the fish has been eaten, the rice will be ready. The traditional way to eat it is to take a fork and dip into the communal fish bowl, and then eat the rice straight from the pan.

PAELLA

Saffron rice (Pictured on page 8) Serves 4–5

Preparation and cooking time: about 1 hour

10–12 saffron threads or 1 teaspoon yellow colouring

6–8 tablespoons olive oil

1 rabbit or 1 small free-range or corn-fed chicken weighing 1–1.1 kg (2–2½ lb), jointed into 16 pieces (see page 67)

4 garlic cloves, sliced

125 g (4 oz) chorizo or paprika sausage, chunked

1 red and 1 green pepper, de-seeded and cut into strips

1–2 medium-size squid weighing 500 g (1 lb) in total, cleaned and sliced into rings

500 g (1 lb) Italian or risotto rice

500 g (1 lb) tomatoes, scalded, skinned and chopped

1 teaspoon paprika

The word 'paella' has its origin in the Latin name for a pan, 'patella', an acknowledgement that it was the Romans who first planted Valencia's rice paddies. In its modern form, the paella pan is a purpose-made, shallow, double-handled, raw-iron frying pan. The governing principal is that the diameter of the pan should be broad enough to accommodate in a single layer the correct amount of rice per person – roughly 125 g (4 oz) per head.

A paella is best cooked over a wood fire, which, when reduced to charcoal, ensures the even cooking of the rice and the proper degree of evaporation of liquid. The key ingredient is the round absorbent 'pudding' variety of rice and its preliminary turning in good olive oil. The traditional Sunday entertainment in rural areas is a paella cooked in the open air, often by the father of the family, with as many of the ingredients wild-gathered as possible. The version I give was my own family's favourite combination: geography dictated the local composition.

If using saffron, leave it to soak in a splash of boiling water for 15 minutes, then squash it down to release the flavour (I put mine in the blender). Lay out all the ingredients within easy

about 900 ml (1½ pints) cold water or chicken stock

125 g (4 oz) shelled peas

12 freshwater crayfish or large prawns, preferably raw

12 cooked snails or fresh raw mussels, or a handful of clams in the shell

salt

reach: timing is of the essence.

Heat a wide, shallow iron frying pan or flat-bottomed wok, or a paella pan with a top diameter of 43 cm (17 inches). Pour in the oil. When it is hot, put in the rabbit or chicken pieces, turning and frying them on all sides. Add the garlic, *chorizo* or paprika sausage and peppers and fry for a few minutes until lightly caramelised. Stir in the squid rings and then the rice. Turn the rice in the oil until all the grains are coated and transparent. Throw in the tomatoes and paprika and pour on the saffron liquid or colouring and as much water or stock as will cover the layer of rice to a depth of 2.5 cm (1 inch). If using a *paella* pan, the liquid should come up to the base of the handle. Bring to the boil, bubble fiercely for 5 minutes and then turn the heat down. Cook gently for 10 minutes. Unless cooking over a fire, keep the rice moving as it cooks.

Stir in the peas and lay on the crayfish or prawns if they are raw. Simmer for 5 minutes and then lay the shellfish on top to open in the steam, with the crayfish or prawns if they are ready-cooked. Cook for 5 minutes and then season to taste with salt. Remove the *paella* from the heat; it should still be moist. Let it rest, covered with a clean cloth, for 10 minutes to allow the rice to finish swelling and the grains to separate. The rice should be moist and succulent.

The traditional way to eat a *paella* is out of the communal cooking pan itself. Put an inverted plate in the middle and balance a dish of salad on top (cos lettuce, tomatoes and onions, salted and dressed with lemon juice and olive oil). Everyone then eats the section nearest to them; the rice under the plate keeps hot for second helpings. Serve with plenty of fresh bread.

Leftover *paella* makes excellent little croquettes: bind with egg, shape into little cylinders, roll in flour, coat with egg and breadcrumbs and deep-fry. Lovely with a fresh tomato sauce (such as the one served with fritters on page 50).

ONE-POT DISHES

Spain has a wide variety of these excellent soup–stews, often called after the cooking pot in which they are most characteristically prepared. Providing a perfectly well-balanced meal in one dish, with the minimum of fuss and all the juices preserved in the cooking liquor, they are the most popular everyday meal throughout the country. Each region of Spain has its own variations, mostly based on one of the pulses and including spiced sausages, black puddings and wind-cured salt ham, with the rest dictated by availability and local preferences.

Leftover pulses are delicious as a *refrito*: fry the remains in a little oil and simmer until the liquid evaporates and the base forms a hard, crisp crust; stir the crust in several times and continue to fry until dry and crumbly. Delicious served Mexican-style with a fried egg and a tomato chopped with chilli. Save leftover broth to make Croquetas de Jamón (Ham croquettes, page 12), or one of the soups on pages 19–22.

OLLETA AMB AL I OLLI

Beans and vegetables with garlic sauce — Serves 4

Preparation time: 4 hours soaking + about 45 minutes + 2–2½ hours cooking

500 g (1 lb) butter beans, soaked for at least 4 hours

1.2 litres (2 pints) water

4 tablespoons olive oil

1 bay leaf

500 g (1 lb) spinach, shredded roughly

1 garlic clove

2 tablespoons paprika, or 3 dried red peppers (nõras), torn into pieces

This is a springtime version of an aromatic stew from Spain's Levante region: it has no meat, but meat, fish and salt cod can be added to it. It takes its name from the earthenware casserole in which it is usually prepared. In Valencia, the chilli used is the small, plump, scarlet 'guindilla', or 'little cherry', a nickname it shares with the village policeman. Canned butter beans can be used if you prefer: you will need two 439 g (14 oz) cans.

Olleta amb Al i Olli (Beans and vegetables with garlic sauce)

1 fresh or dried red chilli, de-seeded

2–3 spring onions, chopped

grated zest and juice of 1 lemon or bitter (marmalade) orange

500 g (1 lb) new potatoes

1 teaspoon salt

4 medium-size tomatoes, scalded and skinned if wished

4 slices of bread

1 quantity of Al i Olli (Garlic and oil sauce, page 56)

Drain the beans and put them in a large saucepan with the water, oil and bay leaf. Bring to the boil, turn down the heat, cover and leave to simmer for 1½–2 hours, until the beans are soft.

Stir in the spinach, garlic, paprika or dried red peppers, chilli, spring onions and lemon or orange zest and juice. Bring back to the boil and add the potatoes, enough boiling water to nearly submerge them, and the salt. Bring back to the boil, turn the heat down and cook for 15 minutes, until the potatoes are nearly done.

Remove the chilli from the broth and chop it up with the tomatoes. Toast the bread, Spanish-style, on a grill over a flame or on an electric ring turned down low. This quick blister-blacken gives a special caramelised flavour.

Strain the vegetables and beans from the soup and transfer them to a warm, deep dish. Put a slice of toasted bread into the bottom of each soup plate and pour in a ladleful of soup. Serve the soup first with the tomato/chilli handed separately, followed by the vegetables and beans with the Al i Olli. A fine juicy Valencian orange completes the meal perfectly.

LENTEJAS CON CARNE DE CERDO

Lentils with pork — Serves 4–5

Preparation time: 30 minutes + 1 hour cooking

2 tablespoons olive oil

2 garlic cloves, crushed

250 g (8 oz) pork shoulder, cubed

1–2 carrots, chopped

500 g (1 lb) brown-green lentils

250 g (8 oz) bacon misshapes

a short length of black pudding (optional)

Lentils do not need soaking and only take an hour to cook, which makes them the fast-food of the pulse tribe. The tiny brown or larger greeny-brown lentils are an ancient crop round the Mediterranean, and they are the ones used in Spain. The orangy-yellow lentils used to make Indian dhal are not suitable.

Warm the oil in a deep saucepan and stir in the garlic, pork and carrots. Let all take a little colour.

Add the lentils and all the other ingredients, except the potatoes and greens or cabbage, and pour in the water. Bring to the boil, turn down the heat, cover loosely and leave to simmer

1 medium-size turnip, chopped

1–2 celery sticks, de-stringed and chopped

6 peppercorns, crushed roughly

1 teaspoon paprika

1 bay leaf

about 2 litres (3½ pints) water

2–3 medium-size potatoes, peeled and chunked

1 head of spring greens or ½ cabbage, shredded

salt and pepper

To finish:

1 tablespoon sherry or wine vinegar

2 tablespoons chopped fresh mint

2 tablespoons chopped fresh parsley

1 teaspoon chopped fresh or dried oregano or marjoram

2 tablespoons olive oil

gently for 40 minutes, adding more water if necessary.

Add the potatoes and continue to cook for another 20 minutes. Add the greens or cabbage, bring back to the boil and cook for 6–8 minutes. Taste and adjust the seasoning. Stir in the vinegar, mint, parsley, oregano or marjoram and olive oil.

Serve the lentil stew in deep bowls, with a robust red wine. I sometimes accompany it with a bowl of *croûtons* fried in olive oil with a few cubes of streaky bacon. A salad, a slice of cheese and some fruit – a juicy orange, or something a bit exotic like a custard apple – completes the meal.

PUCHERO ANDALUZ

Andalucían stew — Serves 5–6

Preparation time: 5 hours soaking + 35 minutes + 1½–3 hours cooking

500 g (1 lb) chick-peas

2–3 thick-cut salted pork belly or unsmoked bacon rashers

½ head of garlic (about 6 cloves)

about 2.25 litres (4 pints) water

This is the most popular dish in the part of Spain in which I brought up my own family. There was no defined recipe, and the puchero might sometimes be nearly meatless, flavoured only with a chunk of ham bone. In my own house, sometimes we served the broth first, more often it was all dished up in a deep soup plate and eaten with a fork and spoon.

2–4 tablespoons olive oil

1 small boiling fowl or roasting chicken weighing 1–1.1 kg (2–2½ lb), preferably free-range, jointed

250 g (8 oz) bacon misshapes (optional)

1 onion or leek, sliced

2 dried red peppers, de-seeded and torn into pieces, or 1 tablespoon paprika, or 1 red pepper, de-seeded and sliced

1–2 links of black pudding (morcilla), sliced thickly (optional)

2 small chorizos or paprika sausages, cut into 7 cm (3-inch) lengths

2 beef tomatoes, scalded and skinned if wished, chopped roughly

1 green pepper, de-seeded and chopped

2 large potatoes, peeled and sliced

250 g (8 oz) greens, chopped, e.g. spinach, chard, cabbage, kale or turnip tops

salt

To finish:

1–2 tablespoons olive oil

2 tablespoons chopped fresh parsley, preferably Italian flat-leaf

Leave the chick-peas to soak in fresh water for at least 5 hours, or overnight.

Cut off the rind from the pork belly or bacon, cut the rind into squares and cube the meat. Do not skin the garlic or separate the cloves, but hold the whole thing in a flame to char the paper covering and roast the cloves a little. Drain the chick-peas and put them in a large, heavy saucepan with the water, oil, chicken (if it is a boiling fowl), bacon misshapes, if used, onion or leek, salt pork or bacon, garlic, and dried red peppers, paprika or red pepper. Bring to the boil and then turn down to a fast simmer. Cover loosely and cook for 1½–3 hours, until the chick-peas are soft but still firm. You may need to add extra boiling water during cooking.

Add the roasting chicken joints if you are not using a boiler. Add the black pudding, if used, *chorizos* or paprika sausages, tomatoes and green pepper. Bring back to the boil and cook for 10 minutes. Add the potatoes and cook for about 15 minutes until the potatoes are nearly soft. Stir in the greens, turn up the heat to return it to the boil and simmer for another 5 minutes.

To finish, taste and add salt and stir in the olive oil and parsley. Drain off the *cocido* broth and serve first, in deep soup plates with plenty of fresh bread. Follow with the meats and vegetables.

FABADA ASTURIANA

White beans with bacon — Serves 5–6

Preparation time: 4 hours soaking + 25 minutes + 2–3 hours cooking

- *750 g (1½ lb) haricot beans, soaked for at least 4 hours*
- *250 g (8 oz) bacon misshapes*
- *250 g (8 oz) streaky bacon or salted pork belly in one piece or bacon joint*
- *2 salted pig's trotters, ears and tail (optional)*
- *2 garlic cloves, crushed*
- *6 peppercorns, crushed roughly*
- *a pinch of saffron threads (optional)*
- *175 g (6 oz) black pudding, sliced thickly*
- *salt*

To finish (optional):

- *a handful of thread noodles*
- *a little chopped fresh parsley*

The beauty of this famous dish lies in the quality of Asturia's plump, buttery white beans. Originally these were 'faba' (broad) beans, the native bean of Europe, but were later replaced with the New World's haricot beans. The fabada is as variable as any of the other beans-and-bones stews of Iberia. Here is the basic recipe, with concessions to ingredients easily obtainable in this country.

Drain the beans and put them in a large, heavy saucepan with the rest of the ingredients, except the black pudding and saffron, if using. Pour in enough fresh water to cover everything to a depth of 2.5 cm (1 inch). Put the saffron threads, if using, in a cup with a splash of boiling water and set aside. Bring the beans and meat to the boil, turn down the heat, cover loosely and leave to simmer gently for 1 hour, removing any scum with a slotted spoon.

Mash the saffron threads and add to the pan with their soaking water. Continue to simmer gently for 1½–2 hours until the beans are quite soft and the meat is tender. Add more boiling water if necessary. Add the black pudding at the end. Taste and add salt if necessary.

Drain off most of the broth and reheat with thread noodles and chopped parsley if wished. Remove and slice the meats. Pile the beans up on a hot, deep dish with the rest of the broth and lay the meats on top. Serve the broth first, followed by the beans and meats.

CHICKEN AND GAME

Rural Spanish housewives usually keep a few hens to eat up the household scraps. The elderly fowl, past laying, go to make a rich strong broth; the young cockerels make a festive dish for high days and holidays. A barnyard fowl is inevitably more muscular and tough than the hen-housed bird, and traditional Spanish cookery takes no risks, jointing it rather than cooking it whole. Battery birds are common, but the Spanish chicken is still a smallish breed.

The Iberian Peninsula is still relatively underpopulated, and stocks of wild game are perhaps less depleted than elsewhere in Europe. Nevertheless, nothing is as plentiful as it once was, and efforts to conserve stocks are now being reinforced by the rearing of table game-birds. Wild game is usually cooked quite simply with wine and herbs.

CODORNICES A LA BILBAÍNA

Quails with parsley and garlic — Serves 4

Preparation and cooking time: 30–45 minutes

- *50 g (2 oz) lard or butter*
- *4 tablespoons oil*
- *6 quail each weighing about 125 g (4 oz), cleaned and halved*
- *125 g (4 oz) fresh breadcrumbs*
- *2 garlic cloves, chopped*
- *4 tablespoons chopped fresh parsley*
- *1 teaspoon chopped fresh or dried thyme*
- *salt and pepper*

Farmed quail provide a succulent replacement for the 'chimbos' – small songbirds – which have always been a favourite snack. In this delicious recipe from Bilbao, butter or lard declares the difference between the olive-oil cookery of the south and the more French-influenced dishes of the north. This is a good way to treat any feathered game or young poultry.

Heat the lard or butter and oil in a heavy shallow pan. Lay in the halved birds and fry gently, turning once, until golden brown all over and cooked right through: 10–15 minutes should be ample. You may need to do this in 2 batches. Remove the birds and fry the breadcrumbs, garlic, parsley, thyme and salt and pepper in the butter and oil which remains. Sprinkle the birds with this crisp, fragrant topping.

Start the meal with a vegetable dish, maybe Pisto Manchego (Vegetable hot-pot, page 44). Finish it, Burgos-style, with Cuajada a la Manera de Burgos (Junket with honey and nuts, page 88).

POLLO CHILINDRÓN

Chicken with red peppers — Serves 4–6

Preparation time: 30 minutes + 1–1½ hours cooking

- *1 small chicken weighing 1–1.25 kg (2–3 lb), preferably free-range or corn-fed, jointed*
- *4 tablespoons olive oil*
- *2 garlic cloves, crushed*
- *1 onion, chopped*
- *1 thick slice of salt-cured ham or lean bacon, diced*
- *2 red peppers, de-seeded and sliced lengthways*
- *1 bay leaf*
- *1 teaspoon chopped fresh or dried thyme*
- *500 g (1 lb) tomatoes, scalded, skinned and chopped, or a 397 g (14 oz) can of chopped tomatoes*
- *chopped fresh parsley (optional)*
- *salt and pepper*

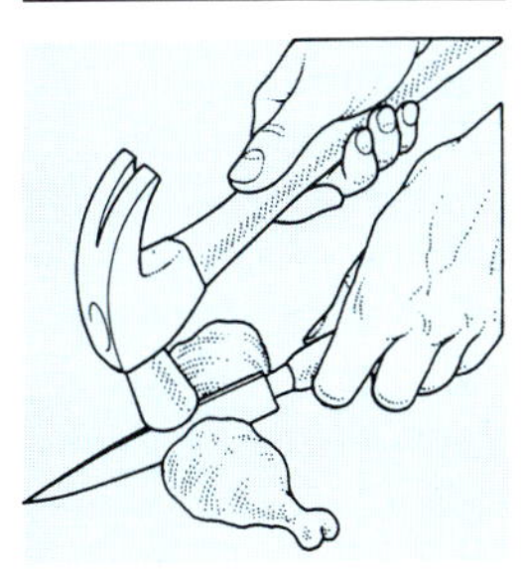

This is a classic dish from Zaragoza in Aragón: the scarlet sauce makes it a pretty dish for a party. The Aragonese also prepare their lamb in the same way. It is even better if made a day ahead, and reheats perfectly.

Joint the chicken further, in the Spanish manner, which includes all the bits. Chop the drumsticks across the bone into 2, thighs into 2, wings into 2, breast into 4. I tap a heavy knife through the bone with a hammer.

Heat the oil in a deep casserole. Add the chicken pieces, garlic and onion. Fry gently until they take a little colour. Push the pieces to one side and add the ham or bacon, peppers, bay leaf and thyme. Fry for a few minutes, stir in the tomatoes and bubble up. Turn down the heat, cover tightly and simmer for 1–1½ hours until the chicken is tender and the sauce well-reduced. If necessary, remove the lid at the end of cooking, take out the chicken and allow the mixture to bubble up and concentrate the juices. Taste and add seasoning. Sprinkle with parsley, if wished, and serve with plain-boiled or mashed potatoes.

OCA AMB PERES

Goose with pears — Serves 6

Preparation time: 35 minutes + about 2 hours cooking

For the bird:

1 young goose or large duckling weighing 2.25–2.75 kg (5–6 lb)

25 g (1 oz) lard or goose dripping

3 garlic cloves

1 bay leaf

For the pears and sauce:

6 small, firm pears

25 g (1 oz) lard

1 onion, chopped finely

1 garlic clove, chopped

1 tablespoon pine kernels or whole-nut peanut butter

1 tablespoon raisins

1 tablespoon finely chopped fresh parsley

1 teaspoon ground cinnamon

1 beef tomato, scalded, skinned and chopped

1 tablespoon milk

300 ml (½ pint) water

75 ml (3 fl oz) anís or anis-flavoured white brandy, or vodka plus ½ teaspoon aniseeds

To finish:

125 g (4 oz) sugar

4 tablespoons water

This is a classic Catalan dish. This version, made with a young goose, comes from Sali in Gerona, where it is the great feast-day treat. The goose is a sure sign of a well-run barnyard: of all domesticated creatures, the goose is naturally the most efficient converter of fodder to meat.

Preheat the oven to Gas Mark 4/180°C/350°F if you are using it.

Wipe the bird and prick the skin all over without going through to the meat. Heat the lard or dripping in a casserole large enough to accommodate the whole bird and turn the bird in the hot oil until it gilds and the fat begins to run. Add the garlic and bay leaf. Cover and cook gently for about 1½ hours, turning regularly, until nicely cooked through. Failing a casserole, you can roast the bird in the oven: prick the skin, rub the bird with the lard, pop the aromatics into the cavity and roast for about 1½ hours until cooked through.

Meanwhile, peel the pears, leaving the stalks on. In a pan with a lid, melt the lard and fry the onion, garlic, pine kernels or peanut butter, raisins, parsley and cinnamon. When shiny and soft, add the tomato and milk and bubble up for 15 minutes until you have a thick sauce. Pour in the water and brandy or vodka and aniseeds and bring back to the boil. Lay in the pears, bring back to the boil, turn down the heat, cover and simmer for about half an hour.

Remove the pears carefully and put them aside to keep warm. Pour the sauce round the goose and simmer for another 20 minutes or so. Bubble it up if the sauce

Oca amb Peres (Goose with pears)
Pollo Chilindrón (Chicken with red peppers)
Pato a la Sevillana (Spiced duck with olives and oranges)

is not thick enough and skim off the fat.

Just before serving, arrange the goose on a plate and surround with the pears, stalk upwards. Pour the sauce round the goose. Melt the sugar in the water in a small pan and let it simmer and caramelise to a walnut brown. Quickly pour a little caramel over each pear. It will harden immediately, but not for long, so do not caramelise the pears until almost ready to eat. Serve with green vegetables.

PATO A LA SEVILLANA

Spiced duck with olives and oranges — Serves 4

Preparation time: 30 minutes + 40–45 minutes cooking

- *1 duck or 2 wild ducks weighing 1.75–2.25 kg (4–5 lb) in total, jointed*
- *1–2 tablespoons seasoned plain flour*
- *4 tablespoons olive oil*
- *1 teaspoon ground cinnamon*
- *½ teaspoon ground cloves*
- *2 garlic cloves, chopped*
- *16 green olives*
- *150 ml (¼ pint) white wine*
- *2 large oranges*
- *1 tablespoon clear honey*
- *salt and pepper*

This is a dish from Seville, at the head of the great basin of the Guadalquivir. The marshes of the Coto Doñana yielded, in the days when it was the fief of the huntsman, fine fat ducks for the pot. The locals like the ducks cooked with olives and oranges – the classic dish, but with a Spanish twist.

Wipe the duck joints and roll them in the seasoned flour. Heat the oil in a casserole, put in the duck joints and let them take a little colour. Throw in the spices, garlic and olives. Pour in the wine and bubble up. Finely grate the orange zest and add it with the honey to the pan juices. Cover and simmer gently for 40–45 minutes, until the duck is tender. Skim the fat from the sauce.

Peel the oranges right down to the flesh and either slice them, or cut out the segments. Add the pieces to the sauce just before serving. Taste and adjust the seasoning.

Serve with a salad of cos lettuce and chopped onions sprinkled with lemon or bitter orange juice, olive oil, salt and chopped tarragon to refresh the palate, Seville-style.

POLLO AL AJILLO

Chicken with garlic — Serves 4

Preparation time: 20 minutes + 1–2 hours marinating + 35–45 minutes cooking

1 small free-range chicken weighing 1–1.25 kg (2–3 lb), jointed

6 garlic cloves, chopped roughly

1 tablespoon chopped fresh or dried oregano or marjoram

½ lemon, chunked small

1 tablespoon seasoned plain flour

8 tablespoons olive oil

150 ml (¼ pint) dry sherry or white wine

salt and pepper

The country housewife's favourite way with a young cockerel, or a rabbit from the rosemary-scented cistus shrub, this simple recipe depends on perfect ingredients. My local baker's wife included chunks of lemon, which gives the dish a rather Moorish flavour. Make it with a free-range chicken: frozen joints do not give the same result.

Chop up the joints into smaller, bite-sized pieces, following the instructions on page 67. Mix with the garlic, herbs and lemon chunks and season with pepper. Leave to take the flavours for an hour or two: overnight is best.

Shake off the aromatics and reserve them. Dust the chicken joints with the seasoned flour. Heat the olive oil in a heavy frying pan or skillet. Add the chicken joints and turn the pieces until they are well browned. You may need to do this in 2 batches. Add the garlic and lemon chunks and let them take a little colour. Pour in the sherry or wine and bubble up. Turn down the heat, cover loosely and leave to simmer gently on a low heat for 35–45 minutes, until the meat is cooked through but still moist and tender, and the juices have practically evaporated, leaving a delicious garlicky oil as the sauce. Season and serve with bread and a salad.

PERDICES CON COL

Partridges with cabbage — Serves 4

Preparation time: 25–30 minutes + 1–2 hours marinating + 45–60 minutes cooking

2 partridges each weighing about 175 g (6 oz), split in half

This is a speciality of the uplands of Lérida, in the north east of the peninsula. It is a countryman's winter dish, perfect for older birds.

1 onion, chopped finely

2 garlic cloves, chopped

150 ml (¼ pint) red wine

4 tablespoons olive oil

1 beef tomato, scalded, skinned and chopped

150 ml (¼ pint) water

2.5–5 cm (1–2-inch) stick of cinnamon

1 bay leaf

1 sprig of fresh thyme

salt and pepper

To finish:

1 small or ½ large savoy cabbage

1 tablespoon seasoned plain flour

1–2 tablespoons olive oil

salt

Wipe the partridges and remove any stray feathers. Put the birds in a shallow bowl with the onion, garlic, wine and salt and pepper and leave to take the flavours for an hour or two, turning once or twice. Take them out of the marinade and shake off the excess liquid. Reserve the marinade.

Heat the oil in a casserole, put in the birds and turn them until they brown a little. Add the tomato and bubble up. Add the reserved marinade, pour in the water and bring to the boil. Slip in the cinnamon stick, bay leaf and thyme. Turn down to simmer, cover and leave to bubble gently for 25 minutes.

Meanwhile, slice the cabbage thickly and bring it to the boil in plenty of salted water. Drain, dust lightly with the flour and fry the slices quickly over a high heat in a lick of oil.

Tuck the fried cabbage slices round the partridges. Bring back to the boil, cover and simmer for 20–35 minutes, depending on the age of the birds, until they are deliciously tender. You may need extra water, and you may like to add a few thin slices of potato with the cabbage.

PICHONES A LA TOLEDANA

Aromatic pigeons — Serves 4

Preparation time: 20 minutes + 50–60 minutes cooking

8 tablespoons olive oil

4 pigeons, cleaned and halved

2 onions, chopped

16 unskinned garlic cloves

175–250 ml (6–8 fl oz) dry sherry

1 tablespoon sherry vinegar

2 bay leaves

1 teaspoon chopped fresh or dried marjoram

A recipe from Spain's high central plateau which was once heavily wooded. Toledo is an ancient ramparted city and remains well-endowed with pigeons. The sharp sauce contrasts deliciously well with the gamy flavour of the birds.

Heat the oil in a heavy casserole, add the pigeons and turn them in the hot oil to seal. You may need to do this in 2 batches. Throw in the onions and garlic and fry until they soften and gild. Pour in the sherry and vinegar, tuck in the bay leaves and marjoram and bubble up. Add salt

Pichones a la Toledana (Aromatic pigeons)

salt and pepper

and pepper. Turn down the heat, cover tightly and simmer for 50–60 minutes, until the pigeons are quite tender. Take off the lid towards the end and evaporate all the juices, leaving the pigeons bathed in aromatic oil.

Serve one bird per person, making sure each has its share of garlic cloves – creamy and gentle-flavoured when slow-cooked like this. Chips or plain-boiled potatoes dressed with chopped onion and parsley will give the meal substance. Accompany the dish with the robust red wine of La Mancha.

PAVO EN PEPITORIA

Turkey with almonds and saffron — Serves 4

Preparation time: 20–25 minutes + 50–60 minutes cooking

1 kg (2 lb) turkey joints

50 g (2 oz) lard or 4 tablespoons olive oil

1 thick slice of day-old bread, torn into pieces

2 garlic cloves, chopped

a small bunch of fresh parsley

2 tablespoons ground almonds

½ teaspoon ground cloves

1 teaspoon ground cinnamon

6 saffron threads, soaked in 1 tablespoon boiling water, or 1 teaspoon turmeric

grated zest and juice of ½ lemon

150 ml (¼ pint) sherry or white wine

1 onion, chopped finely

salt and pepper

The farmyard turkeys of Andalucía have not changed much since the Jesuits brought them over from the New World. They are handsome bronze-feathered birds about the size of a large British chicken, but with much less breast meat. This recipe is for a young bird. The bread-and-almond thickening of the sauce predates the arrival of the turkey by a good few centuries.

Chop the turkey joints into bite-sized pieces – a heavy knife tapped through the bone with a hammer does the trick.

Heat the lard or oil in a frying pan or skillet. Fry the bread and garlic until golden. Toss in the parsley and fry for a moment. Transfer the bread mixture to a food processor or mortar. Process or pestle-pound to a thick sauce, with the ground almonds, spices, saffron and its soaking water or turmeric, grated lemon zest and juice and sherry or wine.

Gently fry the turkey pieces and onion in the lard or oil which remains in the pan, adding extra if necessary. When the turkey is a little browned and the onions are soft, stir in the thick sauce. Bubble up, cover and turn down the heat. Simmer very gently for 50–60 minutes until the turkey is cooked. Add a little more water if the sauce dries out. Season to taste.

Serve hot, with crusty bread. A salad and chips completes the main course. It is also good with rice or noodles.

LIEBRE A LA AMPURDANESA

Hare with chocolate — Serves 4

Preparation time: 30 minutes + 35–45 minutes cooking

- *1 kg (2 lb) hare portions*
- *2 tablespoons seasoned plain flour*
- *125 g (4 oz) streaky bacon, diced*
- *2 tablespoons olive oil*
- *12 pickling onions*
- *125 ml (4 fl oz) red wine*
- *125 ml (4 fl oz) water*
- *4 tablespoons ground hazelnuts or almonds*
- *50 g (2 oz) plain chocolate*
- *salt and pepper*

Chocolate is used here in the Mexican way, to enrich and thicken the sauce: Spain adopted the culinary pleasures of her New World colonies with enthusiasm. Partridge, pigeon and rabbit are also delicious cooked like this.

Remove the fine membrane and chop up the hare portions to give 12–16 small pieces. Roll them in the seasoned flour. In a heavy casserole, heat the bacon with the oil until the fat runs. Add the onions and let them take a little colour. Remove the onions and bacon and set aside. Add the hare pieces to the casserole and turn them in the hot fat until they seize and brown a little. You may need to do this in 2 batches. Return the onions and bacon, pour in the wine and water and bubble up. Turn down the heat, cover tightly and simmer gently for 25–35 minutes, until the meat is nearly tender. Stir in the nuts and chocolate and cook for another 10 minutes, until the sauce is rich and thick. Taste and add salt and pepper.

Serve with bread to mop up the delicious dark juices. A sharp little salad, maybe with orange in it, will complete the pleasure.

MEAT

Pork is the most popular and widely available meat in the markets of Spain. The omnivorous pig has long been an honoured member of the Spanish rural household. Isolated farming communities still make their own winter supplies of salt-cured ham and paprika-spiced sausage.

Lamb and mutton, being the preferred meat of the Moors, disappeared from the southern menu at the time of the re-conquest until quite recently, although the shepherding uplands of the rest of Spain felt no such inhibitions. Among the rural communities of the south, kid is the preferred meat for any special occasion.

Mature beef is usually stewed. Young beef, darker and more mature than veal, is the preferred meat for grilling and frying. Spanish butchers are adept at boning out and slicing up virtually the whole animal into thin escalopes. The only usual alternative is a piece of shin for enriching the *cocido* (broth).

Town dishes are a little different, with offal as the traditional source of cheap protein for the urban poor, who had no access to the wild harvests available to country people. So recipes for variety meats come from the towns.

CALDERETA DE CORDERO

Spiced casserole of lamb — Serves 4

Preparation and cooking time: about 1¼ hours

1 small shoulder of lamb, chopped into portions through the bone, or 750 g (1½ lb) boneless stewing lamb

75 ml (3 fl oz) sherry

a sprig of fresh thyme

1 bay leaf

Shoulder of lamb is ideal for this slow-cooked, fragrant dish. It can be prepared in advance and freezes perfectly. This is a recipe from Málaga, where Moorish culinary influences remain strong; the breadcrumbs used as thickening would have been familiar to Tudor housewives.

Trim the lamb of fat and cut into bite-sized cubes. Put into a saucepan with the sherry, herbs

300 ml (½ pint) water

2 tablespoons olive oil

125 g (4 oz) lamb's liver in 1 piece

2 garlic cloves, crushed with ½ teaspoon salt

2 tablespoons fresh breadcrumbs

1 teaspoon ground cinnamon

grated zest and juice of 1 lemon

salt and pepper

and salt and pepper, and enough water to submerge it. Bring to the boil, skim and add the oil. Turn down the heat and simmer for 20 minutes. Add the liver (still in 1 piece) and bring back to the boil. Turn down to simmer and cook for 15 minutes. Take out the liver. Test the lamb – if it is not yet tender, leave it to simmer until it is.

Chop the liver roughly and put it in a blender with the garlic-salt, breadcrumbs, cinnamon, plenty of pepper and a ladleful of the cooking liquor from the meat. Process to a thick sauce. Stir the sauce into the meat and its juices. Reheat and simmer gently for 10 minutes.

Remove from the heat and stir in the lemon juice. Taste and add salt and pepper. Serve in individual earthenware casseroles, finished with a sprinkle of grated lemon zest. Accompany with bread to mop up the juices.

ALBÓNDIGAS EN SALSA

Meatballs in tomato sauce — Serves 3–4

Preparation and cooking time: 35–40 minutes

For the meatballs:

300 g (10 oz) minced pork, beef, lamb and/or veal

1 egg

4–5 heaped tablespoons fresh breadcrumbs, soaked and squeezed out

1 garlic clove, chopped

½ large onion, chopped very finely

1–2 tablespoons finely chopped fresh parsley

1 teaspoon chopped fresh or dried thyme

1 teaspoon chopped fresh marjoram or oregano

Making meatballs – moulding the mixture into large marbles – is a lovely task for children: more fun than sand-and-water play, and you can eat the result. The proportion of meat to breadcrumbs can be varied according to the means of the cook. Make double the recipe and freeze half for later. The mixture can also be used as a stuffing for vegetables.

Work the meat, egg, breadcrumbs, garlic, onion and herbs thoroughly together with the salt and plenty of pepper. Work it some more until the mixture is a firm ball of paste. Divide it into 15–18 little balls and roll them lightly in the flour. Heat the oil in a large frying pan. Put in the meatballs in a single layer, in 2 batches if necessary, and fry them gently, turning them to cook all sides, until firm and lightly browned. Take them out and reserve them.

½ teaspoon salt

1–2 tablespoons plain flour

1 tablespoon oil

pepper

For the sauce:

½ large onion, chopped finely

500 g (1 lb) tomatoes, scalded, skinned and chopped. or a 397 g (14 oz) can of chopped tomatoes

100 ml (3½ fl oz) oloroso sherry or red wine

1 bay leaf

salt and pepper

Now make the sauce. Fry the onion gently in the fat in the pan, adding extra oil if necessary, until it softens. Add the tomatoes and bubble up fiercely until you have a thick sauce. Splash in the sherry or wine, add the bay leaf and boil up again for a minute to evaporate the alcohol. Slip the meatballs into the sauce, bring back to the boil, turn down the heat and simmer gently for 15–20 minutes. Season to taste.

Serve the meatballs Spanish-style with thick-cut chunks of bread and chips, or with rice or mashed potatoes.

HÍGADO ENCEBOLLADO

Liver and onions — Serves 4

Preparation and cooking time: 50 minutes

500 g (1 lb) calves' or lamb's liver

6–8 tablespoons olive oil

500 g (1 lb) onions, sliced finely

1½ tablespoons dry or oloroso sherry

salt and pepper

This is a favourite dish of María José Sevilla, author of 'Life and Food in the Basque Country'. It is very simple but quite delicious.

Remove any visible tubes from the liver. Cut it into bite-sized strips, sprinkle with pepper and set aside.

Heat 4–6 tablespoons of the oil in a wide, heavy frying pan. Add the onions and let them cook very slowly for 25–30 minutes, until they are quite soft and lightly caramelised. Remove and set to one side. Turn up the heat, add the remaining oil and throw in the strips of liver. Sauté them briefly, no more than a couple of minutes: they must remain pink and juicy. Return the onions, add the sherry and bubble up for a minute to evaporate the alcohol. Fold all together, season with salt and pepper and serve immediately. It is lovely with mashed potatoes or home-made bread.

OLLETA DE CORDERO

Lamb with ham — Serves 4

Preparation time: 15 minutes + 1½ hours cooking

- *1 small leg or shoulder of lamb weighing about 1.1 kg (2½ lb), boned*
- *½ teaspoon crushed peppercorns*
- *1 teaspoon dried thyme*
- *1–2 thick or 2 thin slices of serrano ham, prosciutto or gammon*
- *100 ml (3½ fl oz) olive oil*
- *250 ml (8 fl oz) dry white wine*
- *2 bay leaves*
- *1 tablespoon paprika*
- *salt and pepper*

This is a party dish, as prepared in Alcoy, a hill town set in the magnificent mountain range behind Alicante. Spanish mountain lambs of the Levante are small, well-flavoured animals, more mature than the milk-fed animals which the rest of Spain prefers. Mountain meat needs rather longer cooking than our plump valley-lambs. The flavours are very concentrated and the meat has a delicious rich flavour.

Preheat the oven to Gas Mark 4/180°C/350°F.

Sprinkle the cut side of the boned joint with the peppercorns and thyme and lay the slice(s) of ham on top. Roll the meat up and tie it into a neat little bolster. Pour a little of the oil into a casserole that will just accommodate the joint and add the lamb. Add no extra salt as there is plenty in the ham or gammon. Pour the rest of the oil and the wine around the joint. Tuck in the bay leaves and sprinkle in the paprika. Bake, uncovered, basting from time to time, for 1½ hours, until the meat is tender and well browned. You may need to add a little water from time to time to stop the dish from drying out, and you may need to lower the heat slightly half-way through cooking.

Taste and adjust the seasoning with plenty of pepper and salt if necessary. Serve the meat, sliced, with its own gravy, and a generous helping of mashed potatoes or plain-cooked rice. To finish, offer sweet white grapes and a piece of honey-and-almond *turrón*, the Spanish *halva* which was a legacy of the Moorish occupation.

LOMO EN ADOBO A LA PLANCHA

Marinated griddled pork fillet | Serves 4–6

Preparation and cooking time: 20 minutes + overnight marinating

500 g (1 lb) pork fillet

3 tablespoons paprika

1 teaspoon dried marjoram or oregano

1 teaspoon dried thyme

1 bay leaf

1 garlic clove, crushed with 1 teaspoon salt

3 tablespoons olive oil, plus extra for greasing

To serve:

rounds of french bread

This fast-food can be bought ready-marinated from the butcher in Spain. Made with the tenderest fillet and well seasoned with its spicy juices, it can be cooked in a moment, ready to be popped into a fresh roll.

Pat the pork fillet dry and rub it with the paprika, marjoram or oregano, thyme, bay leaf, garlic-salt and oil. Wrap it in foil or in a plastic bag and leave it in the fridge overnight at least. It will improve in its marinade for a week.

Pinchitos Moruños (Moorish kebabs)

Lomo en Adobo a la Plancha (Marinated griddled pork fillet)

Slice the fillet into about 12 medallions, on the diagonal if the fillet is slender. Heat a griddle or heavy iron pan until smoking hot. Oil it lightly and lay on the pork medallions. Griddle for 5–6 minutes, turning once.

As soon as it comes off the griddle or pan, lay each medallion on a slice of french bread which will just accommodate it: you don't want to waste any of the lovely juices.

Olleta de Cordero (Lamb with ham)

PINCHITOS MORUÑOS

Moorish kebabs — Serves 4

Preparation and cooking time: 30 minutes + overnight marinating

- *500 g (1 lb) boned pork or lamb, e.g. shoulder, leg, best end or braising, or heart and pig's kidneys*
- *4 tablespoons olive oil*
- *1 teaspoon ground cumin*
- *1 tablespoon paprika*
- *1 teaspoon turmeric*
- *1 teaspoon chopped fresh or dried thyme*
- *1 tablespoon chopped fresh parsley*
- *1 teaspoon pepper*

To finish:

- *1 teaspoon salt*
- *8–12 cubes of bread*

These are the great feria-day treat: no fairground or village square celebrating its patron saint's day would be truly festive without the delicious scent of spicy kebabs grilling over a small charcoal brazier tended by a 'Moor' in a scarlet, tasselled fez.

Trim the meat into cubes no bigger than ordinary dice. Put them into a large bowl with the oil, spices, herbs and pepper and mix well. Cover and leave in a cool place or the fridge overnight.

Thread the meat onto 8–12 skewers, using 6–7 little pieces for each one. Grill the kebabs over a very high heat, turning them frequently, until nicely roasted but still juicy (if you have chosen pork, it will need thorough cooking).

Sprinkle the kebabs with the salt and spear a cube of bread on the end of each. They are lovely with crisp chips and a salad of roughly chunked tomato, cucumber and mild onion.

RIÑONES AL JEREZ

Kidneys with sherry — Serves 2–3

Preparation and cooking time: 30 minutes + 30 minutes soaking

- *375 g (12 oz) calves', lamb's or pig's kidneys, trimmed of fat and veins*
- *1 tablespoon wine vinegar*
- *25 g (1 oz) lard or 2 tablespoons olive oil*
- *1 onion, chopped finely*
- *1 garlic clove, crushed with a little salt*
- *1 teaspoon paprika*

This speciality of Jerez, where fighting bulls are as plentiful as the venerable wine which bears the town's name, is cheap, delicious and quickly prepared. It is also very good made with chicken livers, which will take less time to cook.

Slice the kidney(s) thinly and leave to soak in water mixed with the vinegar for half an hour. For quicker results, sprinkle with the vinegar and then scald with boiling water.

Heat the lard or oil in a heavy pan. Fry the onion and garlic-salt until they soften and take a

2 tablespoons fresh breadcrumbs

1 teaspoon chopped fresh or dried oregano or marjoram

1 bay leaf

4–6 tablespoons dry or oloroso sherry

150 ml (¼ pint) water

salt and pepper

To finish:

1 tablespoon chopped fresh parsley

little colour. Drain and add the kidneys and turn them in the hot oil for a minute or two. Stir in the paprika, breadcrumbs and herbs. Pour in the sherry and bubble up to evaporate the alcohol. Add the water, stir well and bring back to the boil. Cover tightly, turn down the heat and simmer gently for 15–20 minutes, until the kidneys are tender and the sauce thick and rich. Bubble it up for a moment, uncovered, if the sauce needs a little reduction. Taste and add salt and pepper and then stir in the parsley.

I like this in the Spanish manner, with bread, thick-cut chips and a salad of tomatoes, cucumber and onion, with a glass of cold sherry to echo the rich flavour of the sauce.

ESTOFADO DE RABO DE BUEY

Spiced oxtail hot-pot — Serves 4

Preparation time: 20 minutes + 3–4 hours cooking (+ overnight chilling if necessary)

1–2 oxtails weighing about 1.25 kg (3 lb) in total, cut into sections

2 tablespoons olive oil

1–2 slices of streaky bacon, chopped

1 large onion, chopped

2 garlic cloves, crushed with 1 teaspoon salt

1 celery stick, chopped

1 carrot, chopped

1 tablespoon paprika

1 teaspoon ground cinnamon

3–4 cloves

1 bay leaf

250 ml (8 fl oz) oloroso sherry or red wine

salt and pepper

This is a dish common to the old leather-working towns: this version is a speciality of Córdoba. The skins for tanning came in with the tail still attached, and the leather-workers' wives would take advantage of the perk. If you have extra guests, add a can of butter beans or chick-peas.

Preheat the oven to Gas Mark 2/150°C/300°F if you are using it. Trim off the excess fat from the oxtail pieces and remove any stray whiskers.

Heat the oil in a large casserole. Turn the oxtail in the hot oil until lightly browned and then remove and set aside. Put in the bacon, onion, garlic-salt, celery and carrot and fry gently until the vegetables soften. Return the oxtail, add the spices, bay leaf, ½ teaspoon of pepper and sherry or red wine and bubble fiercely for a moment or two. Pour in enough water to submerge all the oxtail pieces. Season, bring back to the boil, turn down the heat and cover tightly. Leave to cook on a very low heat or in the oven for 3–4 hours, until the meat is practically falling off the bones. Check from time to time and add more water if necessary.

Skim off any excess fat. Taste and adjust the seasoning. At this stage it can be left for later reheating, when it tastes even better, or frozen as it is. Or it can be left in the fridge overnight, which makes it easier to remove the excess fat.

Serve with baked potatoes or rice. Or, Spanish-style, with crisply-fried fat chips and plenty of bread, and a plain salad to follow.

GUISO DE VENADO O BUEY

Venison or beef in red wine — Serves 5–6

Preparation time: 20–25 minutes + 1½–2 hours cooking

- *1 kg (2 lb) stewing venison or beef*
- *2 tablespoons seasoned flour*
- *4 tablespoons olive oil*
- *1 slice of streaky bacon or salt-cured ham, cubed*
- *2 garlic cloves, chopped*
- *1 onion, chopped*
- *1 carrot, chopped*
- *1 celery stick, chopped*
- *1 tablespoon paprika, or 1 dried red pepper, de-seeded and torn*
- *½ teaspoon peppercorns, crushed*
- *a sprig of fresh thyme*
- *a sprig of fresh rosemary*
- *1 bay leaf*
- *a few juniper berries or a splash of gin*
- *450 ml (¾ pint) red wine or oloroso sherry*
- *1 teaspoon salt*

This rich aromatic stew is one of my own favourites. It can be made with any of the tougher cuts of meat. It can be prepared ahead, freezes perfectly, and is even better reheated.

Preheat the oven to Gas Mark 2/150°C/300°F if you are using it.

Cube the meat neatly and dust the pieces with the seasoned flour. Sear quickly on all sides in the olive oil in a heavy casserole. Remove the meat or push it to one side and add the bacon or ham, garlic, onion, carrot and celery. Let them fry a little. Stir in the paprika or dried pepper and peppercorns. Tuck in the thyme, rosemary and bay leaf and add the juniper berries or gin. Pour in the wine or sherry and bubble up. Add enough water to just submerge the meat, if necessary, and bring back to the boil. Sprinkle in the salt. Cover tightly and leave to simmer very gently on a low heat or in the oven for 1½–2 hours, until the meat is very tender. Check every now and then and add a little more water if necessary.

Serve with rice or mashed potatoes, and a salad of ripe tomatoes and onions to cut the richness.

Guiso de Venado o Buey (Venison or beef in red wine)

1980

DESSERTS

Spain has such an abundance of fruit all the year round, that meals are usually concluded with something seasonal: honey-sweet grapes, juicy oranges, creamy-fleshed custard apples, ripe figs, scarlet-seeded pomegranates, persimmons, yellow-fleshed peaches, downy apricots or sticky-sweet plums among them. All the summer berries are cropped early and make their first appearance in the warm days of spring. Melons are the great summer treat: great pyramids of watermelons appear by the roadside; or, at the other end of the scale, there are the tiny sweet rock melons of the south. Somewhat perversely, canned fruit in syrup is considered the great treat.

The Moors introduced cane sugar to Europe. Sugar-cane was planted both in Andalucía and the Algarve to supply the Arab taste for sweetmeats and syrups. After the Moorish occupation was over, the Spanish and Portuguese convents in particular continued with the tradition of sweetmaking. The other sweet legacy of the Moors was *turrón*, a delectable almond and honey sweetmeat which is now the traditional Christmas treat all over Spain. Lately white and black nougats and several different marzipans have been added to the commercial range. The closest to the original *halva* is the *Túrron de Jijona*, a kind of nutty brown fudge.

MANTECADOS FINOS

Spiced almond biscuits — Makes about 24

Preparation time: 30 minutes + 35 minutes baking

250 g (8 oz) pure white pork lard, plus extra for greasing

250 g (8 oz) caster sugar

Mantecados are a rich, powdery shortbread made with lard rather than butter. Children love them and hope to find them in their shoes on the morning of the Three Wise Men's visit on 6 January – the day when all good Spanish children are rewarded with presents.

2 egg yolks

grated zest and juice of 1 lemon

500 g (1 lb) plain flour, sieved

250 g (8 oz) ground almonds

½ tablespoon ground cinnamon

Preheat the oven to Gas Mark 4/180°C/350°F.

Soften the lard and whisk it until fluffy with the sugar, egg yolks and lemon zest. Beat in the flour, ground almonds, cinnamon and lemon juice until you have a soft dough. Pat out the dough to a thickness of 1 cm (½ inch) and cut out rounds with a large wine glass. Transfer the biscuits to a greased baking tray. Bake the biscuits for 20 minutes and then turn the oven down to Gas Mark 2/150°C/300°F and let them cook for another 15 minutes until they are pale gold.

Transfer the biscuits carefully to a wire rack to cool – they are very crumbly. When cool, wrap each biscuit in a scrap of tissue paper and store in an airtight tin. They are particularly delicious with a dessert wine, such as the treacle-dark wines of Malaga.

BISCOCHO

Olive oil Madeira cake | Serves 6

Preparation time: 10 minutes + 45–50 minutes baking

3 large eggs (size 2)

175 g (6 oz) plain flour

2 teaspoons baking powder

½ teaspoon salt

200 ml (7 fl oz) light olive oil, or a mixture of sunflower and olive oil, plus extra for greasing

175 g (6 oz) caster sugar

Mediterranean housewives have easier access to olive oil than butter, and use it in many of their cakes and biscuits – perfect for those who are worried about cholesterol. This version has been a family favourite since we lived in Andalucía. It must be the easiest cake ever invented.

Preheat the oven to Gas Mark 4/180°C/350°F. Oil a 1 kg (2 lb) loaf tin and line the base with greaseproof paper.

Whisk the eggs lightly in a small bowl. Sieve the flour, baking powder and salt into a large bowl. With a wooden spoon, beat the rest of the ingredients into the flour until the mixture is smooth and free of lumps. Spoon the mixture into the tin. Bake the cake for 45–50 minutes, until well risen, firm to the finger and shrunk from the sides. Leave in the tin for 10 minutes and then transfer to a wire rack to cool.

CUAJADA A LA MANERA DE BURGOS

Junket with honey and nuts Serves 4

Preparation time: 5–10 minutes + 2–3 hours setting

600 ml (1 pint) full-fat milk

1 teaspoon rennet essence or crushed rennet tablets (available from a good chemist)

Pastel de Naranjas (Almond sponge with oranges)

To finish:

½–1 teaspoon ground cinnamon

4 tablespoons shelled walnuts or hazelnuts, cracked roughly

4 tablespoons clear honey, e.g. acacia, lime or orange blossom

Burgos junket was my children's favourite treat when we were passing through this beautiful cathedral town in northern Spain. The area is known for its sheep's cheese – 'queso de Burgos' – and junket was widely enjoyed, being the first stage in the cheese-making. There they leave the junket to set in little half-glazed terracotta pots, which add greatly to the pleasure. Cow's or goat's milk can be used if you cannot get sheep's milk.

Cuajada a la Manera de Burgos (Junket with honey and nuts)

Leche frita (Frittered milk)

Warm the milk to finger-warmth. Stir in the rennet and pour the mixture into individual pottery jars or glasses. Leave to set in a cool place, 2 or 3 hours will do the trick.

Serve at room temperature, finished with a sprinkle of cinnamon and topped with a spoonful each of the nuts and honey.

PASTEL DE NARANJAS

Almond sponge with oranges

Serves 4–6

Preparation time: 20–25 minutes + 40–50 minutes baking

- *butter for greasing*
- *flour for dusting*
- *1 medium-size or 2 small oranges*
- *4 eggs*
- *175 g (6 oz) caster sugar, plus extra for sprinkling*
- *250 g (8 oz) ground almonds*
- *4 tablespoons rum*

This is an upside-down cake from the orange groves of Valencia. The combination of oranges and ground almonds makes it fresh-flavoured and light as a feather. Serve it as a special treat with well-iced 'agua de Valencia' (dry champagne and fresh orange juice).

Preheat the oven to Gas Mark 5/190°C/375°F. Line a cake tin 16–18 cm (6½–7 inches) in diameter with a circle of greaseproof paper.

Butter and lightly flour the tin and paper thoroughly and sprinkle with a little sugar. Grate the orange zest and reserve it. Pare off the pith from the orange(s) and cut into thin slices, removing any pips. Drain in a sieve, reserving any juices. Lay the slices in the bottom of the cake tin.

Whisk the eggs together until frothy. Sprinkle in the sugar and beat the mixture until it is white and stiff enough for the whisk to leave a trail. This is easiest with an electric beater as it takes twice as long as you expect. It should be pale, frothy and quite thick. Fold in the ground almonds and orange zest. Don't be afraid to turn the mixture well over to 'tire' it. Spread over the sliced orange in the cake tin. Bake for 40–50 minutes, until the cake is well-browned and firm to the finger. Leave to settle for 5 minutes and then tip it out onto a plate. Sprinkle with the rum and any reserved juices from the orange slices.

Note: If the cake is for children, replace the rum with an orange and honey syrup, made by dissolving 2 tablespoons of honey in 4 tablespoons of orange juice. This is also good served as a sauce with the cake.

LECHE FRITA

Frittered milk — Serves 4–6

Preparation and cooking time: 40–45 minutes + 1 hour chilling

For the custard:

- *600 ml (1 pint) milk*
- *25 g (1 oz) butter*
- *50 g (2 oz) cornflour*
- *1 teaspoon plain flour*
- *4 tablespoons sugar*
- *1 egg plus 4 egg yolks*
- *oil for greasing*

For the coating:

- *1 egg*
- *2 tablespoons milk*
- *4–5 bread slices, crusts removed, made into breadcrumbs*
- *oil for frying*

To finish:

- *1 tablespoon sugar*
- *¼ teaspoon ground cinnamon*

This lovely sweet is simply a very thick custard, breadcrumbed and fried. Together with its close cousin Flan (Caramel custard, page 94), it is the pleasure which awaits good Spanish children who finish up their greens. It can be made ahead and fried at the last minute, or reheated in the oven.

Put all the ingredients for the custard in a liquidiser and process thoroughly. Don't worry if the butter makes the mix seem somewhat lumpy. Heat the mixture gently in a saucepan over a low heat. Keep whisking and stirring so that it doesn't stick. Just as it comes to the boil and thickens, turn down the heat and simmer for about a minute to cook the flour. It should be very thick. Spoon it into a lightly oiled 20–23 cm (8–9-inch) square dish in a layer about 1 cm (½ inch) thick. Refrigerate until cold and then cut it into 5 cm (2-inch) squares.

Beat the egg on a plate with the milk. Spread the breadcrumbs on another plate. Dip the squares in the egg-and-milk to coat them and then press gently all over in the breadcrumbs. Heat 1 cm (½ inch) of oil in a heavy frying pan. When it is hot, carefully fry the squares, a few at a time, for about 4 minutes each side, until pale golden. Drain on kitchen paper. Sprinkle with the sugar and cinnamon and serve immediately.

PAN PERDIDO

Eggy-bread with cinnamon — Serves 2

Preparation and cooking time: 20 minutes + 10 minutes soaking

- *1–2 eggs*
- *3–4 tablespoons milk*
- *1 teaspoon sugar*

These make a good substitute for 'churros' to serve with Chocolate con Canela (Drinking chocolate with cinnamon, page 92). My own children found them a great treat for breakfast or tea.

2–3 slices of day-old bread, with or without crusts, cut into fingers

25 g (1 oz) butter

1 tablespoon oil

To finish:

ground cinnamon

sugar (optional)

Fork up the egg with the milk and sugar. Soak the bread fingers for 10 minutes or so in the egg mixture.

Heat the butter and oil in a small frying pan. Fry the fingers, turning once, until crisp. Sprinkle with cinnamon, and extra sugar if you like the crunch.

CHOCOLATE CON CANELA

Drinking chocolate with cinnamon — Serves 2

Preparation and cooking time: 10–20 minutes

397 g (14 oz) can of condensed milk, made up to 600 ml (1 pint) with water, or 600 ml (1 pint) full-fat milk, plus extra for mixing

125 g (4 oz) plain chocolate, broken up

1 short length of cinnamon stick or 1 teaspoon ground cinnamon

1 teaspoon cornflour

To finish:

½–1 teaspoon ground cinnamon

Spain was the first of the Old World to acquire a taste for the New World's chocolate: Montezuma's addictive treat; the best breakfast for lovers. This is the thick, rich brew thickened in the Aztec manner with cornflour, as prepared in Sanlúcar. I remember big steaming bowls of it during festival-time, particularly good with 'churros', the flour-and-water fritters sold hot from the frying-vat in the corner of every market place.

Put the water and condensed milk, or milk, with the chocolate and cinnamon into a large saucepan. Mix the cornflour with a little water or milk. Heat the pan gently, whisking all the while, until the chocolate has dissolved. Whisk in the cornflour. Turn up the heat and let it boil up. Immediately remove from the heat. Still whisking, let it come to the boil again. Remove and repeat a third time. Whisk it some more and remove the cinnamon stick, if used.

Serve it scalding hot, sprinkled with cinnamon. Accompany with Pan Perdido (Eggy-bread with cinnamon, above) or doughnuts for dunking. It is quite within tradition to take it with a thimbleful of brandy or *anís*.

Chocolate con Canela (Drinking chocolate with cinnamon)
Pan Perdido (Eggy-bread with cinnamon)

FLAN

Caramel custard (Pictured on page 9) Serves 4–6

Preparation time: 20 minutes + 25–40 minutes baking

For the caramel:

4 tablespoons granulated sugar

3–4 tablespoons water

For the custard:

600 ml (1 pint) full-fat milk

3 eggs plus 3 egg yolks, beaten

2 tablespoons vanilla sugar, or 2 tablespoons granulated sugar plus 1 teaspoon vanilla essence

This is the only dessert which is to be found on every Spanish family's table and every restaurant menu. Spanish housewives can buy excellent packet versions of it. My own children love it. It can be made a day ahead.

Preheat the oven to Gas Mark 4/180°C/350°F if you are using it.

Make the caramel in a small heavy-based pan. Melt the sugar over a medium heat, stirring all the time with a wooden spoon, until the sugar dissolves and caramelises to a rich chestnut brown. Watch it carefully as it will take only a moment or two after the sugar dissolves and can quickly burn. Add the water off the heat – be careful as it will splutter. Stir over a low heat for 2–3 minutes until you have a thick, dark syrup. Pour this caramel into a 1.2-litre (2-pint) soufflé dish or 4–6 individual moulds and tip to coat the base. If you are quick and skilful, you will not need to use the water.

For the custard, whisk together the milk, eggs, egg yolks and vanilla sugar. Strain the mixture into the single mould, or divide it among the individual moulds.

Transfer the mould(s) to a roasting tin and pour in enough hot water to come half-way up the moulds. Bake the large one for 35–40 minutes until the custard is just set. The small ones will only need to cook for 25–30 minutes. Alternatively, the custards can be cooked in a bath of barely simmering water on top of the stove. Remove, allow to cool completely and chill.

Run a knife round the rim and unmould the custards when you are ready to serve them. They will make their own delicious caramel sauce.

INDEX TO RECIPES

Cover design: Barry Lowenhoff
Cover illustration: Sally Swabey
Text design: Ken Vail
Illustration: John Woodcock
Typesetting: Hands Fotoset, Leicester
Origination: Colthouse Repro Ltd, Bournemouth